THE
FADING
OF
KIMBERLY

KIT CRUMPTON

The Fading of Kimberly
Copyright © 2018 Kit Crumpton

The characters in this book are fictional. There is no relation to an actual person with a similar name.

The Elgin State Mental Hospital is fictional as are events described in this book.

Images from www.istockphoto.com/portfolio/coffeeandmilk

Paper Back ISBN: 978-0-99653-962-3

eBook ISBN: 978-0-99653-963-0

www.KitCrumpton.com

Acknowledgements

I very much appreciate the support, encouragement and information exchange from my friends Denise Plumer, Bob Hall, Angela Bennett, Joanne Bodin, Peter Forbes, and my husband, Bill Crumpton.

Kimberly Luc Weatherspoon

Table of Contents

Prolog

In a space of no-space, in a time of no-time, Universe and Soul conversed within the void.

Soul: "I want to be beautiful and wealthy. I want the best of everything; clothes, mansion, food and people admiring me. I want a grand life."

Universe: "Have you not already had these things?"

Soul: "Not like this. Of course, I've had some of these things, but in the grand scheme of life they were average."

Universe: "The life experience is never average."

Soul: "I seek a different experience of wealth and privilege."

Universe: "Let's take a look."

A fog separated in grand gesture. "Consider this couple. You will be well provided for, but your brother will be mentally infirmed."

Soul: "No, no. That's not it. I want to be the center of attention."

A fog separated. "Here is an unwed mother, whose mate is wealthy. You will be well provided for, but hidden away from society."

Soul: "No, no. I must be the center of attention within my own circle of society."

Universe tried again. They observed Warren Willard Weatherspoon, a big man, broad shouldered, with his beautiful wife, Lucinda.

Universe: "Perhaps this. Mr. Weatherspoon. He's wealthy. His wife is stunning, and she's a talented soprano."

Soul: "That's closer."

Universe: "She dies in childbirth."

Soul: "That's it! That's what I want."

Universe: "You will get lots of material things. Lovers. Excitement. Attention, without too much publicity. People will admire your wealth, station in life and beauty. But caution! You ask for a heavy thing. Not everyone can carry the responsibility of a person having all these amenities. Wouldn't you rather this?"

In grand gesture, Universe separated a fog to a scene. Soul refused to look.

Soul: "No. I want to be born a Weatherspoon."

Universe sighed: "You shall be born as you ask. Remember, you had asked for something like this before."

Soul: "I didn't know, at the time, that I would be beheaded in a public execution commanded by the King!"

Universe nodded.

Soul: "Death was NOT instantaneous. Life lingered for a few seconds."

Universe: "I was there. I heard your whispers."

Soul: "By the way, why was I born with six fingers?"

Universe: "Artistic license. You wanted to be unique. Memorable. You wanted people to know about you in history. After all, you begat one of the greatest monarchs of all time."

Soul laughed: "Indeed, I was memorable. Could you please be a little less artistic this time? Not so political. Not so public. As if a secret, only a few appreciate."

Universe: "Yes. You will have these things, but know—"

Soul interrupted. "that a lifetime is merely a passing vapor in the wind, compared to the eternity of time."

Universe: "Yes. You remember. So, events may not come out as expected."

Soul: "I know. This is what I want."

Universe relented.

CHAPTER ONE

Paradisum

1939

The flower's Edwin had sent her made her smile. It was an apology. Just yesterday they had argued. She had never before seen his face turn red, nostrils flared, fists clenched.

She had suddenly glanced at a blond man. It was a physical attraction and intuitive energy. She could feel him looking at her. She felt his intensity, the blond man, so she simply turned around to see from where the energy came. The wind blew, coming out of nowhere, opening his unbuttoned shirt. Good Lord, his chest and abdomen muscles rippled with every step. His blond hair cut short, square jaw and fair skin made Kimberly think of Hercules. But after the glance, what attracted her even more was the puppy at the end of a leash he held. A Cocker Spaniel. Adorable.

She must have gazed at this human deity and dog a little too long prompting her boyfriend's tremendous reaction.

So sad. She could smell his sweat, soaking his one-piece swimsuit into a splotchy mess. He had just run five miles along the shore of Lake Michigan. His suit and shoes were speckled with dirt and sand.

Her mind had raced, searching for solutions. Should she come on strong and escalate the fight? Or should she speak softly to appease him?

She chose the latter strategy for its simplicity, and so spoke carefully, in a hushed voice, hoping to assuage his wrath.

From under her beach umbrella, Kimberly adjusted her sunglasses down her nose and tilted her hat so she could look directly at him.

"Edwin, go into the water. You'll refresh yourself."

"I don't want to." He gave her an icy stare.

It didn't work. He couldn't hear her words. It was as if he were in his own tunnel vision, dark, ugly, mean and helpless.

"Hmmm..." She considered his reaction, annoyed and thinking it over-exaggerated. She was not his property, and if this was how he felt, then maybe she should end it. For now, decorum must be maintained.

She moved from under the beach umbrella in one fluid motion, tossing her sunglasses onto a towel, and approached him with head slightly tilted, eyes demure. Coyly, she caressed his left arm, and then pressed his left thigh against the inside of her hips, suggesting her desire to straddle him.

Kimberly did not notice the shocked expression of a sun-bathing woman, in her thirties, who watched this scene from a few yards away. Sitting up, she had let her magazine drop to her lap as her mouth opened, full to bursting with unspoken outrage, as she squinted over-top her sunglasses.

Edwin caught the woman's reaction from the corner of his eye and chuckled. Kimberly felt him relax as he turned toward her for an embrace, his eyes softened with desire.

"You have a power over me, you vixen. I can never stay angry with you for long."

Scooping her up into his arms, he carried her toward the lake's edge, as she giggled. Her platinum blond hair hung loose, swayed in the breeze.

Kimberly loved Edwin's intensity for her. His desire to please her made Kimberly feel like a goddess. Her nose lifted slightly and contemplated his face as he marched to the lake.

His raven hair and midnight eyes caused some pause. He wore dark colors, suggesting some mystery to his persona. Athletically built, he had sex appeal. Dashing, like Zorro, without the noble imperative. No, Edwin instead held the element of danger.

Her eye caught the glimmer of the gold, Elgin-made watch he wore and cried out, "Oh, Edwin! Don't get your watch in the water!"

He slowed his steps, then stopped altogether and gently put her down. "Right…"

Pulling her around, so she faced the lake, he wrapped his arms around her waist. Then whispered into her ear, "I'll always treasure my watch. Every time I look at it, I think of you, my darling." He paused, pressing his body against hers. "Have I ever thanked you?"

Delighted, she giggled. This provocative question was often a prelude to making love.

"Yes," she whispered, "but you can thank me again."

He pressed his lips against the nape of her neck and her legs wilted. He held her more closely, as she leaned into him and groaned.

Eyes closed, her inner dialogue gave her assurance.

I am a goddess. I have everything. I am beautiful and rich. I have power over people. I rule Edwin.

* * *

The idea was to have an evening affair for Mr. Warren Weatherspoon's birthday. Kimberly insisted upon cocktails and a lavish dinner.

She planned it as she sat in the drawing room, sipping a bourbon and water from a fine crystal tumbler. She wore a floor-length evening dress, whose sumptuous gold material draped over one end of the couch she adorned. A full-length mink coat was draped over the other end.

First thing: review the guest list. Some were friends of her father from his favorite gentleman's club. Others were notable railroad business associates.

Kimberly added the name, Mrs. Marguerite Lynn Bowles, a British lady, widowed and in her forties, whom her father had met at a party given by the Vanderbilt family years ago. Her father liked her British accent, her manners and intelligence.

Her conversational ability will be a very nice addition to the party.

Of course, she added the name, Mr. Edwin Mullusio. She assigned him to the seat across from her at the dinner table, so she could watch him admire her.

Perusing the list further, Kimberly's eyes settled upon the name, Miss Laverne Walls. She groaned. Miss Walls was Warren's secretary, and Kimberly resented her father's, often made, laudatory remarks regarding Miss Walls intelligence, ability and punctuality. She was also vivacious and quite buxom, with pointed tits that made men wonder about her female anatomy.

Common laborer. She has no business being in our niche in society but Father likes her. My God, sometimes I think he prefers her over me. But, of course, not. She's just an oddity to amuse him. Thinks she's so smart.

A subtle pain deep inside her almost made Kimberly wince knowing that '*intelligent*' was not a word Warren would use to describe his own daughter,

Maybe I should place her somewhere between Edwin and one of dad's railroad associates at the far end of the table away from dad.

Kimberly paused, her mind racing over people's names and faces.

I almost forgot, Matthew Keller.

Kimberly met him at her tennis club. A college professor of history, Mr. Keller had strong political slants, but also such uncanny charm that people did not get upset with a point of view that could otherwise be perceived as inflammatory.

I can count on Matthew to add colorful entertainment and a challenge for Father.

Satisfied with her list, Kimberly rang the bell to call the butler. A minute later, William appeared in the room.

"Yes, Miss Kimberly."

"I've modified the guest list and added three more people. Please make sure we have enough food and drink for them."

"Of course, Miss Kimberly. Is there anything else?"

"Yes, please make sure we have Edwin's favorite champagne for dessert. We should have several bottles."

"We have five bottles, Miss Kimberly."

"Good. That should be enough. Thank you, William."

They heard a knock at the front door.

"I'll get the door, William. It's Edwin. We're going to the theater."

William nodded and left the room, as Kimberly rushed to open the front door of the mansion.

"Edwin!"

"Hi, Kimberly!"

Edwin stepped into the mansion, looked around to see if they were alone, then took her hand and pulled her closer for a soft, sensual kiss. Kimberly swooned.

"You look wonderful!" he exclaimed, stepping back and taking both her hands as he gazed at her gown and yellow diamond necklace. She waited, smiling, while he took it all in. "You are like Venus. No... more exquisite."

He stepped forward again, sniffing. "What's that perfume?"

Before she could answer, his lips touched her neck and she felt his tongue caress her skin, downward toward her shoulder. She flushed, wanting, and sucked in her breath. His hand cupped a breast, and her hands clutched at his winter coat. Then, suddenly she let go of him, took a step back and regained her composure.

Her sultry eyes said, "*I want you*", yet when she spoke, her words belied her feelings. "Shouldn't we get going?"

"Of course! We don't want to be late for the show." Edwin gave her a greedy smile and took a step back, placing his feet solidly at shoulder-width.

Her head turned towards the drawing room. Edwin followed her gaze and saw the coat on the couch. He fetched the garment, and helped her slip into it. When he opened the door, a blast of cold December air hit them hard in the face, so they quickly descended the three steps off the front porch and hurried to the car parked in front of the mansion. Edwin, helped Kimberly gather her rippling golden dress and lavish mink coat inside the vehicle, and then rushed to the driver's side.

Sitting alone for those few moments was just enough time for her to validate Edwin, internally.

God, he's sexy! I am so in love with him. And he adores me.

CHAPTER TWO

The Weatherspoon Party

December - 1939

A week later, the Weatherspoon house was all a hubbub, as William made final preparations for the birthday evening festivities.

William, exceptionally suited for his job as the family butler, was an effeminate man who enjoyed working in the lavish Weatherspoon environment. William loved providing creative accoutrements that spoke to the perception of family nobility. This was William's calling, to make things tidy and harmonious by using rigid adherence to the expectations of high society. He was also a confidante; balancing boundaries with dexterity, knowing what to say, when to say it, and those things that should never be said.

Cocktails were served in the drawing room. A bright fire in the fireplace made the room cozy. The room's layout was amended to accommodate fourteen guests. There was a couch, a coffee table and several cloth covered chairs with small tables scattered here and there.

The liquor bar had a variety of spirits: gin, bourbon, whiskey, vodka, rye, and rum. Ice, kept in a pewter bucket, sat behind the bar and below glass shelves that held crystal glasses and tumblers. The cut crystal bounced the fire's light, making the glasses sparkle and wink with prisms of color. A decorated tankard, holding four after-dinner liqueurs, was set at the end of the bar, along with pewter liqueur glasses. The hired bartender stood at the ready to create any desired concoction.

A violinist and a cellist were playing in a corner of the large, two-story entry-way, where a dramatic curved stairway led to the second floor and a balcony. Solid black and white floor tiles were laid in a diamond pattern provided pleasing acoustics.

As guests entered the Weatherspoon mansion, William and a maid collected their coats and hats and showed them to the drawing room, where Kimberly and Warren stood ready to greet them.

The bartender was soon quite busy, and the room smoke-filled, as people lit cigarettes gripped in various styles and lengths of holders.

The conversation was light, due to the constant interruptions as new party-goers arrived. Some people knew each other and gravitated toward acquaintances, while others had to be introduced.

Such was the case with Professor Matthew Keller. Kimberly, her left arm wrapped around his right arm, announced, "Everyone, this is Professor Keller. He teaches history at the University. Please make him feel welcome and introduce yourselves." She then led him to the bar.

Mathew ordered a gin and tonic, as Kimberly whispered, "Let me introduce you to Mr. and Mrs. Harrington. Mr. Harrington is in the banking business."

Drinks in hand, she escorted Matthew to the couple.

"So, you teach history, eh?" Mr. Harrington tucked his chin, so he could look at the Professor's face over his spectacles. "What kind of history? Early American? WWI?" He fingered his thick mustache, turning gray while he scrutinized the professor.

Kimberly excused herself and stepped away to greet another guest, Miss Laverne Walls, who arrived without an escort. Warren saw her as well but took a moment to watch Laverne remove her mink coat and give it to William. Kimberly had nearly reached Miss Walls, when she saw her father hurrying across the room. She stepped back, unnoticed.

Absurd the way Father fawns over her.

Laverne wore a pink silk gown draped across her front so that the folds of the material lay charmingly just beneath her collar bones. Her arms were bared, except for a three-strand pearl bracelet she wore on her right arm. The floor-length skirt had a side slit that showed her calf.

Kimberly considered Laverne's hairstyle.

Overdone curls. Ridiculous! God, the people I tolerate for Father's sake!

Warren put his arm around her small waist and led her to the bar. He enjoyed the feel and the smell of an attractive woman as he held her close to him.

Then, Edwin appeared in the entryway. Kimberly waited a few seconds, watching him remove and give to William his topcoat, hat and gloves. Instinctively, he ran his right hand over his raven hair as he headed for the drawing room.

Kimberly rushed to meet him. *My Dark Prince!*

"I'm so glad you're here," she told him, smiling.

He straightened his tie, raising his nose higher, so as to look down at her.

"Of course, my dear. You look splendid." He looked her over slowly, taking in her rich red dress of crepe material that complimented her marble white skin and platinum blond hair. The neckline was suggestively low cut and one could make out her small breasts when the eye traveled down the neckline to admire the two-carrot, pear-shaped diamond necklace she wore.

The dress hugged her body, considered stylishly indecent by some in conservative circles. Kimberly didn't care. She wanted people to look at her.

She giggled and took his hand. "Let's get a drink for you."

They headed for the bar, passing by Warren and Laverne. Edwin thought he was being discreet when he did a double-take at the voluptuous figure wrapped in pink silk. He shifted his attention to Kimberly.

"Stunning diamond, my dear. Is it a blue diamond?" he asked.

"Yes, it is."

Edwin knew blue diamonds, extremely rare, were very much coveted in higher social circles. He turned his head towards the guests.

"Whose here, my love?"

Kimberly followed his gaze. "That's Professor Matthew Keller talking with Mr. and Mrs. Harrington. Matthew is a history professor and Mr. Harrington is in the banking business. And over there with Father is Miss Laverne Walls and Mrs. Marguerite Bowles. Laverne Walls is Father's secretary."

"I see. How do you know Mrs. Bowles?" Edwin asked.

Kimberly thought, *Hmm, why does Edwin care?* She replied, "She friends with the Vanderbilt's. Father occasionally does business with them and they introduced Mrs. Bowles to Father."

"And who are the people chatting over there?" Edwin's eyes indicated further in the corner of the drawing room.

"That's Mr. Benjamin Fairless with his wife, Jane, and their son Blake and his date, Ellen Glenn."

Edwin considered the family. The ladies were sitting in the corner next to a curio cabinet containing delicate figurine dolls adorned in Dresden Lace. The men stood nearby.

Blake and Ellen must be in their twenties, same age as Kimberly and me.

"What's Mr. Fairless's business?" he asked.

"He's a steel executive."

Hoity-toity folks here.

"Oh, here comes Mr. and Mrs. Tresling. He's a lawyer. Let me introduce you." Kimberly took Edwin's hand and headed towards the newly arrived couple.

Harold Tresling saw Kimberly coming towards him with a handsome man in tow.

She's always beautiful – to a fault! Who's that man with her? He looks familiar.

Kimberly, gay, "It's so nice to see you, Mr. and Mrs. Tresling! Thank you for coming. Let me introduce you to Mr. Edwin Mullusio."

Edwin bowed slightly to Mr. and Mrs. Tresling. "How do you do?"

Tresling, a thin, tall man in his forties with a receding hairline slightly clicked his heals and nodded back. "Fine, thank you."

Mrs. Tresling, her hair pined back under a small evening cap and wearing a black evening gown remarked, "Kimberly, you are extraordinarily beautiful, and what an evening! I'm so glad you invited us."

Kimberly blushed with pleasure. "I'm glad you're here, too. Let me show you to the bar and then I'll introduce you to people."

While Mr. and Mrs. Tresling followed Kimberly, Harold racked his brain over Edwin.

That man with Kimberly. Dashing. Where have I seem him before?

CHAPTER THREE

Dinner

December - 1939

Later, at the dinner table, the guests were finishing their meal as William ensured their glasses were full with their individual intoxicating libation. They relaxed, feeling warm and jovial, the conversation easy. The soft sound of a single violin played in the background. Candlelight danced within the room.

Warren and Kimberly were pleased to see people having a nice time, and with the meal half-eaten, saw that the mood had changed. Now, there was a need for more interesting conversation, away from superficial pleasantries.

"Nasty business, this war," Blake Fairless said.

"Yes, did you hear the Russian's have attacked Finland?" Laverne asked.

"Well, I for one, think taking the Rhineland from Germany was too harsh. It's always been part of Germany. All that did was incite the Nazis," Ellen Glenn whined. She brushed a wisp of her red hair away from the face.

Kimberly saw Professor Keller clench his right hand, resting on the dinner table near his cocktail glass. His eyes looked sad as he caught Kimberly's gaze.

"We must be sensitive to our differences in political discussions, don't you think?" Kimberly fluttered her eyes, looking at each guest. "After all, the war is on the other side of the world. Anyone need their drink refreshed?" Her attempt to soften the conversation was ignored.

The Professor lifted his empty wine glass, making eye contact with the butler. William took a bottle of fine red wine to him and filled his glass. Kimberly also lifted her glass for replenishment.

Mr. Harrington turned toward Warren Weatherspoon, fork in hand, after spearing it into a succulent piece of steak. "Mr. Weatherspoon, what do you think of all this war business? Do you think we'll be drawn in?"

Kimberly seethed inside. *Stupid war! Who cares? It's so far away.* She sighed audibly.

Edwin glanced at Kimberly with an expression that made her feel tingly inside. She saw his eyes travel to her breasts, her necklace, to her lips and eyes. Then he tipped his wine glass to her and took a sip. She smiled back and softened.

You like my dress don't you, Edwin? I wish you could be all over me right this minute.

She looked at her food contemplating Edwin's hands and mouth on her breasts.

As Mr. Harrington chewed his bite of steak, Mr. Weatherspoon drank from his wine glass, then said, "Eventually. It will depend upon how far the conflict reaches other parts of the world. It will be prudent for us to prepare."

"Do you think Germany will go into France?" Laverne asked.

Edwin made eye contact with Laverne. "Not if the Maginot Line holds," he responded. "When I was in Paris a few months ago, the French government believed it was still strong."

Ellen asked, "What's the Maginot Line?"

Edwin explained, "It's a wall; a concrete fortification built to protect France from potential enemies in the east. Germany is one of those enemies."

Kimberly tilted her head considering Edwin's explanation. *You are so gallant, Edwin.*

Mr. Harrington wiped steak grease off his mustache and pulled off his wire-rimmed glasses, looking Warren in the eye. "But what if it doesn't hold? You are right, Mr. Weatherspoon. If a world war starts, our young men will be called into the army. They'll need to be transported on your railroads, won't they?" There was a gleam in his eye.

"Yes, and they'll need some of your money, Mister Banker."

Most of the guests chortled at the jokes, even though the subject was serious. Blake Fairless and Professor Keller were more stoic, the conversation more serious for them. The Professor, cutting into his steak, paused, looking at Mr. Weatherspoon. He was remembering the author, Matthew Josephson, who wrote The Robber Barons.

What's wrong with these people, counting their profits before we even get into the war?

Mrs. Harrington looked at Mrs. Bowles, a buxom, round woman with thick gray hair decoratively piled on top of her head. "I'm sorry your country is at war, Mrs. Bowles. Do you know people who are in the fight?"

"Not yet. Our problem, Mrs. Harrington, is the English Channel is not wide enough to separate us from our enemy should Germany invade France. I'm sure our military watches our shores. After all, it's only been about three months since the war started."

"Yes, the Nazi's are just starting," Mrs. Fairless added. "I cannot believe they invaded Poland."

"German politics has changed since the Great War." Laverne added. "This is why my parents left Germany."

"I'm curious, Miss Walls," Mrs. Fairless asked, "specifically, why did your family leave?"

"I'm Jewish, Mrs. Fairless. My parents saw the rise of antisemitism and so we left before it became a serious difficulty for us. We still have family in Germany and we worry for them."

An awkward pause wafted over the dinner guests as each person reflected upon this new information.

Kimberly thought, *Oh gawd! No wonder she doesn't fit in!*

Mrs. Fairless, *Oh gawd! Why did Warren hire her? Did he know she's Jewish?*

Mr. Fairless, *Good decision they left in time.*

Blake Fairless, *So what if she's Jewish? Look at my mother's face! Embarrassing.*

Ellen Glenn, *A Jew! Really?*

Edwin observed the tell-tale expressions around him. Mrs. Bowles and Mr. and Mrs. Tressling continued eating as if nothing was happening.

Professor Kellor added, "My great-grand-father was Jewish." There was no response.

Warren broke the pause and lifted his glass to Laverne, "The German's are known for their ability and punctuality. It's their loss you left."

Laverne looked back at him and laughed coyly. "It's nice to be appreciated."

Kimberly, irritated, fingered her blue diamond. *Father is making a fool of himself.*

"How about you, Professor? What do you make of all this war business?" Mr. Harrington was still holding his wire-rimmed glasses.

"It's a conundrum, for sure. I imagine Prime Minister Chamberlain feels terrible about being drawn into Hitler's deceit. I'm sorry for that, Mrs. Bowles."

Mrs. Bowles sipped her wine. "Yes, that is unfortunate," she said.

"What deceit?" Kimberly asked, holding her glass of wine.

Laverne answered. "After Hitler became dictator of Germany, he built up his military while he talked peace to his neighbors."

"I confess my daughter lives in her own world. I probably indulge her too much." Warren pushed his chair further back from the dinner table and motioned for William to light his cigarette.

Kimberly looked down at the napkin laid across her lap. *Father still thinks of me as a child. No matter. Edwin knows I'm a woman.*

Mrs. Bowles added, "Even Prime Minister Chamberlain visited Adolf Hitler and Hitler convinced our Prime Minister of his peaceful intentions. I'm afraid we were duped."

She bit into her bread. Suddenly, her eyes went wide, her face red. She grabbed her throat and choked, unable to breathe. Laverne reacted quickly, got up from her chair, hastened behind Mrs. Bowles, pushed her forward and gave her a firm whack on her back.

A wad of bread launched from her mouth and landed on her plate. Mrs. Bowles was able to breathe again. Her face, grateful, as she turned her head to Laverne and leaned back against her chair, "Thank you!"

"Better, huh?" Still concerned, Laverne said, "That was scary. I'm glad you're okay."

Mrs. Bowles' expression was one of relief. "Yes, oh yes." Then she turned her face to the guests, "I am so sorry."

"Don't be," Warren reassured her as Laverne made her way back to her chair.

William moved behind her and gestured, "Let me refresh your plate, Mrs. Bowles."

"Yes, thank you," she replied then smiled at the dinner guests. "I don't want any more bread, please." Her expression mirthful.

The guests laughed. Some lifted their wine glasses as a toast to Mrs. Bowles. There was a slight pause before the tone of the party resumed.

Kimberly looked at Edwin sitting across from her and caught him glancing at Laverne. Edwin detected that, smiled at Kimberly, and concentrated on the last bite of his steak.

Why is he looking at her and not me? Laverne can't compete.

Kimberly asked, "I noticed your bracelet, Miss Walls. Where did you get it?"

Laverne swallowed before she spoke. "My parents bought it at Tiffany's in New York when they came to America. They wanted to mark a new future with something my mother could wear. She gave it to me when I graduated from college." She paused. "I noticed your necklace. It's beautiful."

"Yes, I think this is my favorite. It's rare and very expensive."

Kimberly posed for this moment when all eyes were on her. *Finally, Laverne recognizes she is out of her element in this party.*

Professor Keller, internally seething about profiteering of the wealthy, chimed in. "About the war, Mr. Weatherspoon, what do you think would be Mr. Vanderbilt's business strategy? Or that of the Morgan and Rockefeller empires?"

Mr. Benjamin Fairless, the steel executive, was shocked at the implication made by the Professor. *That's brash!*

Warren Weatherspoon's hackles went up, but he maintained decorum. The meaning behind Professor Keller's questions did not escape him. These were some of the famed "robber barons" of the nineteenth century, whose wealth created the Americanized-royalty of the twentieth century. Fiscal success is sometimes held in contempt by those not so fortunate.

"Interesting question," he responded. "Big business, Professor Keller, is something of a game, like billiards. The competitors innovate and strategize. There is the element of chance and understanding of the critical elements, like physics in billiards. In the national and international arena, the critical elements are politics, assets and economics. There are no apologies if one wins in the game of business."

"Well said," Mr. Harrington offered.

The Professor, a little nervous, plodded on.

"I see your point, Sir. You make it sound so simple. How does one go about maintaining a sense of fair play, when your opponent may not follow the same rules of the game? Consider the Vanderbilt's…"

Only two people at the dinner table were aware of Warren Weatherspoon's association with Vanderbilt III. The butler and the banker. It was Warren's secret that he sometimes earned his money through unscrupulous business deals with Vanderbilt.

He probably doesn't know. Pure coincidence.

Warren took a long, slow draw on his cigarette, and then closed his eyes as he exhaled smoke.

"The term *'fair play'* is a subjective concept. I consider it *'fair play'* if my business dealings are profitable."

His guests laughed. The Professor pressed on.

"But, hypothetically, Sir, is it possible for an American business to profit from a company…let's say…in Germany, during a time of international war?"

Mr. Fairless coughed uncomfortably before Warren spoke.

"No. That would be viewed by Congress as treason. But, to your point, the difficulty comes when American business produces a product that is of interest to a foreign country, who *is* at war. These are complicated concerns, addressed by lawyers and politicians. I'm just a simple steel and railroad man." Warren smiled at the Professor, tipping his cigarette ashes into a silver ash tray.

"Professor," Laverne said, laughing, "it doesn't matter what you say or how you approach it, Warren always has an answer."

Laverne's eyes met Edwin's, who smiled back at her.

Kimberly, "Well, Miss Walls, my father is a successful business man and your employer."

Edwin thought, *Good God!*

Laverne turned red. "Yes, and I appreciate being associated with his enterprises."

Warren watched the two women sitting at opposite ends of the table.

Both beautiful. I wish I could see the soft elegance, the grace that her mother had, in my daughter. Laverne handled that well.

Suddenly it occurred to Harold Tresling where he had seen Edwin Mullusio. It was a picture in the Chicago Tribune where Edwin and a man named Tony Accardo were looking at the Michigan Avenue Bridge.

I hope Edwin Mullusio is not associated with the mob. That could potentially be another difficulty for Warren and another thing for me to handle. I wish Kimberly wasn't so willful.

Mr. Harrington quickly offered, "Let's toast Mr. Weatherspoon for a fine dinner, excellent libations and entertaining dinner conversation. May you have many more birthday celebrations!"

Warren Weatherspoon nodded his head, tipped his glass to his guests, and then took a drink.

"Thank you all. This evening has been my pleasure. Thank you, too, Kimberly."

"Happy birthday, Father."

CHAPTER FOUR
After Dinner
December - 1939

Before long the guests started to leave. William retrieved everyone's coats and hats while the guests chatted amongst themselves as they prepared for the cold winter weather.

Kimberly and Warren stood by the double doors, bidding each person goodnight as they left. Edwin and Laverne, standing in the dining room entryway, stayed behind sharing a chat.

Edwin asked, "Sprichst du Deutsch?" [Do you speak German?]

Laverne replied, "Ein bisschen." [A little bit.]

"Ah, so how did your parents come to America?"

"That's a long story but an interesting one."

"Shall we get a drink in the drawing room while you tell me about it?"

"Sure."

Edwin put his arm around Laverne's waist and led her through a path of people saying their goodbyes to their hosts.

The bar tender had left so Edwin helped himself behind the bar and made a drink.

"I'm making a scotch on the rocks. What can I make for you?"

"I'll have a some more wine, please. Red."

Edwin found an opened bottle of red wine. "Will a Cabernet do?"

"Yes, please."

He poured a glass and handed it to Laverne. "Let's sit over here," he motioned to the couch.

Soon they were engrossed in conversation and laughing, the flush of consumed alcohol warming their faces. Their half-filled glasses were sitting next to a silver cigarette box and lighter on a coffee table in front of the couch.

Warren and Kimberly entered the room.

"Anyone for a game of cards?" Kimberly asked.

Faces close together on the couch, Edwin whispered to Laverne, "Willst du carten spielen?" [Want to play cards?] They both broke into laughter as if a joke had been told.

Kimberly felt the pain of being left out. She cocked her head, expression snippy, one hand on her hip.

"I'm sorry," Laverne said. "Edwin just said something really silly. No thank you. I think I'd best go home now."

Edwin immediately stood to help Laverne up from the couch, but Warren stepped around the small table, and offered his hand to Laverne.

Kimberly watched as both men stumbled over each to help her. *I can't believe this! They should be paying attention to me!*

"Come with me, my dear. I'll get your coat and see you off."

Laverne smiled and took Warren's hand. "It was such a lovely evening," she told him. "I enjoyed the conversation, the food, the wine. Thank you for including me."

Taking Warren's arm, she looked over her shoulder as she walked away, and gave her good-byes to Edwin and Kimberly. Warren put his arm around her waist to steady her and noticed when she brushed her breast against him. They left the drawing room and walked onto the black and white tiled entryway, stopping midway.

"Wait here, while I get your coat and gloves," he said.

Momentarily left alone, Laverne turned and gazed at the huge painting of Mr. Warren Weatherspoon. She took in his dark eyes, thick brown hair, combed back, and fair complexion. His broad shoulders and husky build, so masculine; a man in a man's world. Her eyes scanned the other images in the painting.

I see the symbolism, the moving train in the background, the watch and the Bible. But there's something else...to the left, in the tree...what is it?

She took a few steps toward the front doors to take a closer look at the painting from another angle.

Ah. It's there in the leaves, nicely camouflaged, the head of Zeus cleverly depicted with branches and foliage; thick wavy hair and beard, Roman nose, broad forehead. It's Zeus looking at Mr. Weatherspoon. She smiled. *I wonder if anyone else has noticed.*

Suddenly, Warren appeared with her gloves and mink coat, so she turned and took her proffered gloves, before Warren helped her with her coat.

"May I walk you to your car?"

"Oh no. I parked close to the front door. I'm fine."

Warren opened the front door, and Laverne bid Mr. Weatherspoon a good night.

Meanwhile, Kimberly sat on the couch next to Edwin, where Laverne had been.

"What were you laughing about, Edwin?"

Edwin, annoyed with Kimberly's behavior toward Laverne, managed a reassuring expression.

"I forgot once you entered the room, my dear." He smiled at her, stroking her cheek. "You, my blond goddess, are above ravishing. I will always worship you."

Satisfied, Kimberly reached for a cigarette from the cigarette box and, gazing into his eyes, murmured, "I love it when you make love to me."

He smiled back, still stroking her cheek. She sat back. "Edwin, let's go away. We could fly to the Florida Keys or San Francisco for a few days."

He stopped stroking her cheek and shifted his seat. "That would be nice, but I can't. I have business affairs to attend to."

"What business affairs, Edwin? Tell me." She placed the unlit cigarette on the table.

"I can't say. Really. In fact, I have a long day tomorrow, so I'll say goodnight to you now."

"Oh, Edwin, please stay longer."

Just then, Warren poked his head into the drawing room.

"I'm going to bed now. Good night, Mr. Mullusio. Good night, Kimberly."

"Sleep well, Father."

"I'm leaving also, Sir. Good night. It was a splendid evening."

Warren left the room and they heard him ascending the staircase.

Getting up from the couch, Edwin reached for Kimberly's hand.

"I'll call you first thing in the morning. I promise."

Kimberly walked him to the entry way.

"Where are my things?"

"I'm sure William has gone to bed. Your hat and coat must be over here."

She walked to the door underneath the winding staircase, opened it, disappeared for a moment and came back holding Edwin's hat and coat.

"Here you go."

Edwin donned his coat and hat, then grabbed her roughly, and wrapping his arms around her, kissed her passionately.

"Goodnight," he whispered into her ear.

Then, he was gone.

She hesitated gazing at the closed front door. A feeling of loss - something not right – came to her mind.

The booze must have gone to my head. Edwin is mine.

She turned to make her way for bed satisfied the evening had been successful.

Edwin skipped down the three front steps and onto the walkway, heading for his car parked on the curved driveway. As he passed a small

Ford Anglia he paused, seeing Laverne in the driver's seat. He bent over and tapped the window.

Laverne laughed and rolled it down. "Hello, Edwin!"

"Would you have another drink with me?"

Laverne hesitated. "I don't know, Edwin, it's late."

"Aw, come on. We won't be long. It's Saturday. You have tomorrow off, right? And I'd like to get to know you better."

"Well, alright, just for an hour."

"Great. I'll meet you at Marty's on Fifth Street, about ten miles from here. Know the place?"

"Sure..." She hesitated, then added, "I'll follow you."

She waited as he got into his black Ford Model 91, and then followed him as he pulled down the drive. Minutes later, arriving at Marty's, they found side-by-side parking spots.

Time passed. Lights, music, special rum cocktails and slow dancing. Too much drinking and laughing.

They were both surprised when they awoke the next day, in Laverne's bed.

CHAPTER FIVE

Resurae (Dumped)

1939-1940

Warren woke up late the next morning feeling refreshed and ready to start the day. He thought about last night as he showered and dressed.

I don't like that man, Edwin. He's too suave, almost artificial, and I know nothing about him. Good looking, though. I can see Kimberly's sweet on him. There's something about him though. Too intelligent. That's it! Cunning... Apparently, he does a lot of things well.

Can't say anything to Kimberly. Too headstrong. She'll pick a fight. Nope. I'll figure this out as events unfold. The time will come to say something.

It was Sunday, a day of rest. Warren planned to work part of the day from his home office, then spend his evening with Mrs. Marguerite Bowles.

I'll talk to Marguerite tonight. She'll tell me how to handle this.

Theirs was an agreement. She, willing to perform duties as a temporary stand-in wife. He, providing the watchful eye of a man with political power and plentiful financial resources. Marriage was out of the question, though he knew she secretly desired to be his wife. He was a cautious man, and kept his idiosyncrasies private.

* * *

Kimberly waited a week for Edwin to call her.

Messages from boarding school days. A woman calling a man? Unacceptable! It just isn't done. A man finds a woman unattractive if she throws herself at him. No. Demure is the way to go. Men like women who are reserved.

Kimberly absentmindedly dug her little fingernail into the skin under her thumb nail while she waited for Edwin's call. Over time, she became angry and dug at her skin so vehemently blood was drawn.

She looked for things to do for distraction; a movie, a concert, a tennis lesson.

Finally, he called.

"Hello, my Goddess! I've missed you! How are you? Have you missed me?"

"Edwin, of course I've missed you. You promised to call me. What have you been doing?"

Edwin winced at her tone, knowing from experience it meant he would need to distract her.

After all, she's a spoiled brat with a woman's charm and lots of money.

"Working, my dear, and I'm exhausted. It's a beautiful day though, so why don't we spend it shopping?"

"No, really, Edwin, what KIND of work were you doing?"

Edwin thought, *Gawd, doll-face!* He compared Laverne to Kimberly. *Laverne is mature, educated, self-assured but has no wealth. She's fun to be with. Kimberly is someone I have to work at. Demanding.*

Out loud he told her, "Business transactions. Boring but lucrative. And I'd like to get my mind off it. How about that shopping spree? It's a gorgeous day!"

Kimberly relented. *Does sound boring. I want to be with him.*

"What a lovely idea! There are things I'd like to buy."

Delightful anticipation replaced annoying anxiety. She was so happy to spend her day with him.

"I'll pick you up in an hour, Darling. We'll go downtown, peruse the shops and I'll treat you to lunch."

"See you soon!" *Click.*

She ran to her clothes closet to dress for her date. While perusing through her garments, she caught her image by the corner of her eye, and stopped to closely examine her face. She leaned into the mirror's surface. Her blond hair fell in waves along her slender neck as she examined her eye makeup and lipstick. Kimberly reached for her bottle of Chanel No. 5 and dabbed her shoulders and wrists, and then placed the bottle back on the closet shelf.

I'm radiant. Perfect. Sigh.

The afternoon was unusually warm for January. They enjoyed themselves, absorbed in a shopping spree with no care for expenditures. Kimberly found nice jacket and tailored trousers for Edwin. She felt so womanly, as if taking care of her man and dressing him according to her tastes.

By mid-afternoon they headed for the Weatherspoon mansion. Kimberly had the butler take her parcels to her bedroom while she placed Edwin's things in the drawing room. Her father, having heard the commotion, walked to the drawing room. When he entered, he saw packages on the coffee table, Edwin sitting on the couch and Kimberly at the bar preparing their drinks.

"Hi, Father!"

She hastily greeted Warren with a hug and a kiss on the cheek then went back behind the bar.

"We just returned from shopping. I can't wait until you see the new dress I bought. Edwin helped me pick it out."

Warren bristled inside. He masked his true feelings with a smile for Kimberly's sake knowing she had been smitten by Mr. Edwin Mullusio.

"That's fine," he said.

"And I bought Edwin a couple of things that I liked - a jacket and trousers. He looks so handsome in them!"

Mr. Weatherspoon cleared his throat and glanced at Edwin.

"I hope you enjoy them," he replied haltingly.

"May I get you a drink, Father? How about a soda and bourbon? That's what we're having."

"Yes, thank you."

Then Mr. Weatherspoon turned to Edwin. "How about you and I enjoy a game of billiards? We can have a private talk while Kimberly puts her things away."

"Yes, Sir. I'd enjoy that."

Kimberly placed a crystal tumbler into her father and Edwin's hands. The brown liquid caught the lamplight through each tumbler, expertly cut, so that it bounced waves of light through the bourbon.

"Okay, then. I'll take my drink upstairs while you men have a nice chat." She smiled at them, fetched her drink from the bar, exited the room and headed upstairs.

"Come with me, Mr. Mullusio. You can leave your items in the drawing room. The billiard room is just down the hall. We have a bar there as well, so we can refresh our drinks while we play."

"Thank you," replied Edwin.

Kimberly headed for her bedroom to accessorize her new dress, put her purchases away and change her clothes into something more casual. She considered inviting Edwin to stay for the evening.

I want dad to know him better. Dinner. Just the three of us. Maybe... just maybe... they're talking about me right now.

About an hour later, Kimberly heard the front door close and a car pull away from the Weatherspoon Mansion.

She ran from her bedroom, looked over the balcony railing, and not seeing Edwin, ran down the stairs, through the entryway, into the dining room, and to the large windows, where she pushed aside the curtain just in time to watch Edwin drive away.

Why didn't he say goodbye to me?

Releasing the curtain, she headed to the drawing room to see if Edwin had taken his packages. They were gone.

Kimberly was shocked.

What happened? Was it something between Edwin and Father?

She decided to wait, too afraid of what Warren might tell her, if asked.

Edwin hastened from the Weatherspoon mansion and entered his black Ford Model 91, threw his parcels on the passenger's seat, started the engine and headed down the curved driveway.

Pennies from heaven! Five grand!

He stopped the automobile and checked the traffic before he turned onto the public street.

God, that dame, Kimberly! She's a half-portion, for sure. She'll get over the kiss-off.

A sexual urge passed through him as he considered Laverne's breasts and hips. The nights they spent together. Her personality.

We're on the same page. Not the way I felt when I was with Kimberly.

He stopped the automobile at a stop light.

Laverne. Now there's a dame with a brain! We can make tracks on what I got today. At least until the money lasts.

* * *

A week went by for Kimberly with no word from Edwin.

He's done this to me before. Could it be I'm losing him? Why? I'm everything. Maybe something has happened to him? No. Not likely.

Oh, our love-making was so good. I can still smell him. The power when he's on top of me, my legs wrapped around his waist. His thrusting. I love his passion for me! The way he kissed every inch of my body. Surely, he wants me as much as I want him. After all, I'm a goddess!

Something has happened.

Does he think I'm a loose woman? No. Who does he think he is? Doesn't he realize who I am? I can't let him have the upper hand.

A second week passed without word from Edwin.

This is too much. I'm going away. When he calls me, it's better that William tell him I'm off somewhere. I need to go to a place where I'm appreciated; where there's fun; to be gay.

When Warren came home later that day, Kimberly asked her father if she could go to Hollywood, California to visit his sister, Elenore.

"I need to get away, Father."

They were standing in the entryway, where William was helping Warren Weatherspoon take off his coat and hat. Observing her father's expression, she sighed, and then took a deep breath.

"Father, did you and Edwin have words? He hasn't called me for a couple of weeks."

He looked into her eyes. "No."

She wasn't sure if he was telling her the truth, but there wasn't a way to call his bluff. She knew her father would have no patience with her if she pressed him further.

"I think it's a good idea that you visit Elenore. Go shopping, go to parties, meet movie-stars, have fun. I'll give her a call and tell her that you're coming."

"Thank you, Father." She turned and headed up the stairs to her room to pack. She thought about Elenore while choosing her garments.

Good place to attend parties under the watchful eye of Aunt Elenore, though, she does drink too much. She sure knows a lot of important people and she knows how to have fun.

I'll be so busy I won't have time to think of Edwin. Let him call. I'll be gone.

Two days later, Kimberly boarded a private plane bound for Hollywood.

Aunt Elenore, a woman in her fifties with red-dyed hair, and donning a mink shawl that covered the top of her black dress, met her at the airport with news of a party. They were invited to the home of Director Ernst Lubitsch – that *very* evening – and Greta Garbo would be there!

Kimberly was whisked off into the fast lane of Hollywood elitist society, amongst the who's-who of a community where she did not belong. She was relaxed when she arrived with her Aunt at the Lubitsch mansion. This lifestyle was familiar. The difficulty of belonging presented itself when she entered a room full of people she did not know. She tried her best to participate in captivating conversation, but missed the subtle nuances of an unfamiliar business outside her education and experience.

One can only gush, "You were wonderful in Ninotchka" so many times.

Following the lead of Aunt Elenore, she consumed copious amounts of liquor. Kimberly's preference, wine. Aunt Elenore's preference, scotch.

The liquor provided much needed warmth and courage.

She now moved around the party effortlessly, joining small groups of people, and introducing herself along the way. She found that Mr. Lubitsch's guests were not interested in her, but appreciated a willing ear to their own stories. So, Kimberly deduced her primary contribution to the success of this party was to listen to others and look beautiful.

Out of the corner of her eye she watched the lovely Greta Garbo, taking note of how the actress moved gracefully, so polished. There was an air of aristocracy about her. Extraordinary.

Everything seemed to go well that evening until Aunt Elenore, drunk, grabbed a man's crotch, while clumsily whispering in his ear her desire for a spontaneous coupling in the cloak room. Her overzealous gestures caught the attention of the man's date, who responded at first with a shocked expression, and then outright laughter when it was clear the poor woman was beyond her alcoholic capacity. Laughter can be spontaneous, and like a wave, can quickly waft from ear to ear as the story passed from guest to guest.

"Time to go home," the host announced as he wrapped his arm around her waist and ushered her to the butler, who was standing near the front door with her coat draped over his arm.

Kimberly ran toward her Aunt. "I can take her home, Mr. Lubitsch."

The butler left briefly and retrieved Kimberly's coat.

"I'm so sorry…"

"Don't worry, my dear," Mr. Lubitsch said. "Just make sure she will be alright."

"Of course." She extended her hand and bid him goodnight. The butler held the front door open for the ladies and stared after them as they staggered to their car. Kimberly struggled with the weight of her Aunt, who leaned her one hundred-sixty pounds against Kimberly's small frame. It was dicey. Clumsy.

There was a moment when the butler thought they would not make it. He gasped when they tipped too far, so engrossed in the spectacle that his own muscles wrenched and flexed as if he were part of Kimberly's body.

Woops! That was close. I may have to help.

They made it to the car unscathed. Kimberly helped her Aunt to her seat, entered the driver's side and drove away.

The butler retrieved a handkerchief from his jacket, dabbed his brow and closed the mansion front door.

When they got home, the maid came to Aunt Elenore's aid.

"She's ill," Kimberly explained.

"I'm perfectly fine," Elenore quipped. "Thank you, Kimberly, I'll see you tomorrow morning."

"Good night, Aunty." She walked to her own room, head pounding. Before she closed the bedroom door behind her, she heard Aunt Elenore in the living room muttering, "Where did I put the bourbon?"

The next day, hung over, Kimberly rested at her Aunt's home. She did not see Aunt Elenore until afternoon lunch, when Kimberly explained her nausea. Her Aunt urged her to drink a concoction made with herbs and tomato juice. Kimberly did not know there was a shot of vodka in it.

"I'm meeting friends tonight at the Oasis Lounge for dinner and drinks. Want to join us? We'll get a taxi this time." Elenore took a bite of her chicken.

Kimberly thought about it. "No, thank you. I'm just starting to feel better. I didn't sleep well last night, so I'd rather turn in early."

"Do you mind if I go?"

"Of course not."

That afternoon, Kimberly made plans to fly back home.

She did not see Aunt Elenore the next day. The maid explained that her Aunt had spent the night at a friend's apartment.

"Please tell her I've gone back to Illinois," she told the maid. "I'll call her when I get home."

William met her at the Weatherspoon mansion entry way.

"Hello, William. Did Edwin call?"

"No, Miss Kimberly. Welcome home."

"Thank you." She sighed.

If he doesn't call me, I'll just swallow my pride, hunt him down and ask him why he shut me out. This is ridiculous.

No. I'll give it another week.

Maybe he doesn't love me anymore.

Then, she caught herself.

Stop. I know I'm everything he wants.

* * *

A few days passed. Kimberly pulled her car into a parking space in front of a bookstore and started to walk through downtown Libertyville for her appointment with a seamstress. The road was wide enough for two-way traffic and parking along the sidewalks that bordered store fronts. The stores were two and three stories high, Victorian architecture, and painted different colors of that style. Trees had been planted every few yards, bare now from a January frost.

Further down the boulevard, Kimberly could see the church steeple of the Episcopal church.

It was then that she spied Edwin's black Ford Model 91 parked to the side of the road across the street.

He must be around here, somewhere.

Looking about, she finally saw him. He was with Laverne, entering a restaurant. She waited a couple of minutes wondering what to do. Decision made, she crossed the street and entered the premises. She found them sitting next to each other at a table in the far corner of the room. Their coats were laid out on a chair directly across them, partially hidden underneath the table.

Shenanigans.

She could make out his chin, as if hiding behind Laverne's soft profile. Her chin was down, loose hair forward. Edwin was kissing her neck, her eyelid's fluttering.

That's my man! His lips should be on my neck!

Kimberly walked to them.

"Edwin!"

He looked up, startled. Laverne looked at her, and then looked at Edwin in surprise. Kimberly noticed Laverne's left arm wrapped around Edwin's right arm, her left hand interlocked with his right hand. The gold wrist watch caught a glimmer of light.

That's the watch I gave him!

Edwin swallowed hard, and then relaxed.

"I might as well give it to you straight and fast. Your father doesn't approve of me, Kimberly. It may come as a shock to you, but he paid me off. You're too immature, anyway, my little Golden Goddess. A tad clingy."

Laverne's expression was incomprehensible to Kimberly; something of a mixture between mocking and sadness for a "little-girl" woman being given bad news. Pity.

A rage welled up in Kimberly. She ran out of the restaurant and to her car, where she kept a pistol in the glove compartment. Blinding tears washed down her cheeks. Then she headed back into the restaurant holding the pistol close to her breasts, her hand covering it. No one expected her to be armed. No one noticed what she was holding. They only saw her anguished expression, revealing the depth of her pain.

She walked straight to Edwin and Laverne's table.

POP, POP, POP!

Someone screamed.

* * *

Judicial court was held in the spring of 1940. It was particularly humid.

A pivotal moment occurred during the trial when the detective took the stand. It was all so clear. A lover's quarrel. Edwin called it off, because he had taken up with Laverne Walls.

The prosecuting attorney then called Kimberly to the stand. The court room was packed with folks from the community. After all, this was a salacious affair that tantalized imaginations.

She wore a modest black dress accessorized with a gold chain that held a large ruby stone cut like an hour-glass, intended to accentuate the color of her ruby lips. Few observers missed the unintended symbol of a black widow. Her face, her demeanor, calm and composed. High-heeled shoes ensured that her hips moved provocatively as she walked to her seat in the witness box, chin held high like the actress, Greta Garbo.

"Miss Weatherspoon," Prosecuting Attorney Mr. McHough asked, "how far were you standing from Mr. Mullusio and Miss Walls when you pulled the trigger?"

"About five feet."

The coroner had already testified to a clean, quick kill between Edwin's eyes and Miss Walls, the heart.

"And when Mr. Mullusio and Miss Walls both died, what did you do next?"

"I put my gun on their table, went to the bar and poured myself a whiskey. The bartender had skedaddled."

A gasp came from the courtroom. Some members of the jury chuckled at the word "skedaddled" while they thought, *"I'm sure he did!"*

This was testament to the internal fortitude of the defendant, who had an ice-cold heart, was calculating and convinced of her own infallibility.

More questions. Kimberly talked about confusion in the restaurant as people darted out the door. The police were called by a store proprietor across the street. About thirty minutes later, the police arrived and Kimberly was arrested.

"And you never left the room?"

A momentary expression of confusion with eye brows furrowed passed over her face.

Why would he even ask me this question? Isn't it obvious Edwin chose a common laborer over ME?

Her expression changed, more matter-of-fact. Her back straightened and nose lifted as she looked at the attorney, Mr. McHough, and stared straight into his soul.

"No."

It wasn't too long after that when the prosecuting and defense attorneys made their closing remarks. Then the jury left the room to deliberate the evidence. They took twenty-minutes before they filed back into the court room to give their decision.

"We the jury find the defendant, Miss Kimberly Luc Weatherspoon, guilty of the murders of Mr. Edwin Mullusio and Miss Laverne Walls."

Before court adjourned, the judge announced sentencing to be scheduled for next week.

CHAPTER SIX

Birth Of A Narcissist

1915

Kimberly was born the daughter of Mr. Warren Willard Weatherspoon, a wealthy man from the railroad business, and of Lucinda, an opera performer blessed with a superb soprano voice. Warren courted Lucinda, enticing her with his wealth. Eventually, she agreed to be his wife, knowing she would have a life of luxury and privilege. This suited her needs as a dainty woman, prone to frailty. The theater had been physically demanding and she needed a haven of earthly heaven.

Lucinda's pregnancy was difficult. She feared future birthing pains, unassured that she could survive the physically demanding experience.

It was May 10, 1915 when the pains started. Concerned, Mr. Weatherspoon had the butler, William, call the doctor.

"He's on his way, Sir."

Sitting on a couch in the drawing room reading the newspaper, he acknowledged the butler with a nod. He did not want to be too far away from the bedroom where Lucinda lay, giving her some privacy.

Lucinda's blond hair was pinned up, revealing her long, slender neck. Her face was contorted with pain. She bit her lower lip with perfect white teeth and little blood and spittle dripped down her chin.

The force of the birthing pains took her breath away, overcoming her energy. She could not fight it. She could not work with it. When her cervix finally dilated to ten centimeters, she screamed out loud. The baby started to move down the birth canal.

The nurse did her best, giving Lucinda commands to make the birthing easier. Lucinda never heard her. The nurse continued to monitor her and the baby.

Alerted by the sound, Warren raced from the drawing room, up the winding stairs and bolted into the room to rush to her side. What he saw took his breath away, partially because he had never seen a birth before, but mostly because Lucinda looked so pale. Taking her hand, he saw that her breathing was too labored. Reaching for her wrist, he felt her racing heart and watched the tell-tale signs of excruciating pain on her face. The force overcame her.

A sudden, wide-eyed expression was stamped on her face, mouth gaped open, hand clutching her chest. The baby took her first breath, as Lucinda choked out her last.

Warren sat back. The nurse checked her heartbeat. She was gone. It happened so fast; too fast for the doctor's arrival.

Warren held Lucinda's hand while the nurse wrapped the child in a warm blanket. He wept.

Oh, My God! My dear Lucinda, how can this be happening?

Both hands covered his face as he sobbed. The nurse placed the newborn in the crib.

Memories flooded his mind.

Yesterday morning breakfast – she looked so well! Happy. Sleep, my dear wife. Our baby will be well provided, my dear wife.

Warren turned his head toward the crib when the new-born cried out. He got up from the edge of Lucinda's birth-bed and took a few stiff steps to gaze at his child. He stirred inside, as he considered his life, which would never be the same. He pondered this sensation as he gazed down at the fresh bundle of human infancy.

Here is the future. Hmmm, a heavy responsibility. I will give my child everything, to make up for not having my beloved Lucinda.

The nurse moved to Lucinda's birth-bed and lifted a sheet to cover Lucinda's body. Then she turned to watch Warren Weatherspoon gaze at the infant. He unfolded the wrapping to make sure of the baby's gender. She waited, giving Warren time to collect his thoughts.

A girl. Why couldn't it be a boy? Someone I could teach. Someone I could hand over my legacy.

He re-wrapped the blanket around his daughter.

She's so beautiful. Angelic. Perfect. I will give her everything. She will want for nothing.

Warren shifted his eyes towards the nurse.

"Please bring the butler."

He wanted a moment of privacy while he adjusted to providence.

The nurse left the room, then stopped at the balcony overlooking the large entryway of the black-and-white-diamond-patterned tiled floor. She hoped she would get a glimpse of William, but didn't, so she rushed down the winding stairs, and then went to the door underneath the stairwell. Passing through, she went along the hall of closets, to the kitchen at the end. It was there she found William having a late bite to eat. She knew sometimes William did not have a chance to eat a meal, and so he found sustenance during odd periods of the day.

"William, Mrs. Weatherspoon has died. Mr. Weatherspoon needs you in the master bedroom."

William nodded his head, swallowing the food in his mouth as he got up from the kitchen table. Dabbing his lips with a cloth napkin, he made his way to Mr. Weatherspoon.

He paused at the bedroom door, softly knocking.

"Come in, William."

"I'm so sorry, Sir."

A knock came at the front door, made by one of the heavy, lion-faced door knockers on the massive, double front doors of the Weatherspoon mansion.

"That must be the doctor. Excuse me, Sir, while I show him in."

William descended the winding stairs to the first floor and opened the left side of the double front door.

"Welcome, Dr. Dodson. Mrs. Weatherspoon has passed. She's in the bedroom. First door to the right." William pointed up the stairs after he took Dr. Dodson's coat and hat.

Holding his doctor's bag, the doctor ran up the stairs and entered the room, taking in the drama of Warren standing next to the crib with Mrs. Weatherspoon's body covered by a white sheet.

He nodded to Mr. Weatherspoon as he made his way to Lucinda's body, removing the white sheet to examine her. When he finished, he replaced the sheet, turned to Warren and walked to the crib to examine the baby. He removed the blanket and gently handled this miraculous blessing of new life.

"Well, Sir," he said, turning to Warren, "The baby looks fine. I'm sorry for your loss, Mr. Weatherspoon." Turning to practical matters, he added, "You'll need to keep a nurse for your new daughter. I have several recommendations for you. Meanwhile, the nurse you presently have will do nicely. If you are interested, we can ask if she can stay."

Still looking at the baby, Mr. Weatherspoon nodded his head.

"I'll call for an ambulance to move to the body to the morgue."

Again, Warren nodded his head in silence.

Dr. Dodson felt awkward. "Do you have any questions?"

Warren shook his head.

"Fine then. I'll leave you, Mr. Weatherspoon. Don't hesitate to call if there's anything else I can do for you," the doctor said, and then left.

Warren wondered, *I know how to run a business. I don't know how to mother a daughter. Guess I can hire the right people. It will work some-how. It has to.*

A soft knock. The nurse came in.

"Mr. Weatherspoon, I can stay and help you with the baby as long as you need me."

"Thank you."

And then, "Excuse me." Warren Weatherspoon left the room.

CHAPTER SEVEN
Perinde Obliterato (Ignoring)
1919

Warren's business kept him fully occupied, absorbed in the complexity of a rolling stock and steel businesses. New enterprises popped up. Others failed. Predicting on demand needs. The pulsation of railroad building, railroad trains, electric trains, and automobiles. Iron girders for tall building construction and bridges. Innovative patents that changed materials, gadgets and processes. Sometimes they worked, other times they failed. Financial stock fluctuations. The rise of corporate unions. And local and international events that affected everything.

High risk. Fast paced. It truly was a man's world. Predatorial. Bordering on reprehensible, but always exhilarating.

* * *

A few years passed and Kimberly became a toddler. Warren liked the name Kimberly, an old English name that rolled easily off the tongue.

New nurses came and left. Each had their own personalities and stories. They'd leave for marriages, demands of WWI, and moving on to better employment.

While they all loved and nurtured the baby, they observed a young life with too much change. She never connected to a consistent female provider. And Warren, obsessed with his business, paid little attention to her.

One day, William overheard a conversation between two governesses discussing the Weatherspoon daughter. One was leaving, the other taking on her old position. They were in the kitchen sitting at a long table. William was checking the wine and liquor stock in a walk-in closet nearby.

"I don't know what will happen to this child. She has everything but heart."

"I agree. She's so privileged in circumstances, yet needy."

"That's it! She's needy. Good word!"

"Yes. It feels as if she negotiated with God, demanding her birthright into the Weatherspoon household and God relented, giving her exactly what she had asked."

A chuckle and a sigh. "How insightful. Are you a gypsy?"

The other laughed. "No gypsy blood in my family, but I do tend to be intuitive. Underneath, the child is starving. It's so sad."

"Yes, it is."

As he listened to this exchange, William privately agreed with them, then turned his attention to a re-count of the bottles of Pinot Noir.

Morning. Warren Weatherspoon sat at the dining room table, a plate of eggs, sausage and grits before him. The newspaper, propped up on a stand, as his eyes bore into the articles he was reading.

William, dressed in his butler uniform, stood discreetly behind Warren, waiting for his master's command.

Masticating voraciously, Warren lifted his coffee cup for William to refill. After taking a sip, he set the cup on the saucer, grabbed the newspaper, and snapped it open to select the next article to read.

He was particularly interested in the deliberations happening at the Paris Peace Conference, which heralded the end of the Great War (WWI), and how the powers were working to realign the geography of countries in Europe.

Keeping abreast of current events was a critical element to Weatherspoon's railroad business. It helped him predict the future with a convincing level of accuracy and make successful business decisions. While reading, he detected early morning sunlight through curtain sheers behind him, where he sat at the far end of the dining room. On each side of the sheers hung heavy drapes of ornamental brocade from Italy.

Warren glanced up at William.

"Has Josephine left?"

William nodded.

Warren appreciated the company of Miss Josephine Lyle. She accommodated his needs and was very much aware of Warren's boundaries; a kept woman.

The men heard footsteps coming down the winding staircase. It was the nanny carrying Kimberly, dressed in a pink ruffled frock, her blond hair tied back with a pink ribbon. The nanny wore a black and white uniform of servitude.

They entered the dining room. Warren looked up from his plate as the nanny carried Kimberly to Warren hoping the father would reach out to the toddler and place the child on his lap.

"We've come to say good morning, Sir."

Warren wrapped his hand around the child's white shoe, a lace stocking top spraying overtop the shoe, and shook it as if he were shaking a lady's hand.

"Fine, just fine," he said.

Kimberly squirmed away to turn and look over the nanny's shoulder. Her back was to Warren. The nanny looked at Mr. Weatherspoon, hesitated a moment, then asked, "What would you like to do for her birthday, Sir? She turns four next week."

"We'll have a party. Just me and the baby."

The nanny knew what that meant. It would be a brief affair, since the toddler made Warren uncomfortable and he didn't want a gaggle of women and children in his house.

William broke the silence. "I'll make the arrangements, Sir."

"Thank you, William."

Warren stood up from the table. The nanny interpreted his action as a dismissal.

"We'll have our breakfast now, won't we?" she said, using baby-talk, and giving Kimberly a slight bounce before walking toward the entry way and heading to the kitchen.

William followed them partway, intending to fetch Mr. Weatherspoon's coat and hat, which he brought to Warren, then helped him get into his coat.

"William, buy birthday presents you think the baby will like."

"Yes, Sir."

William opened the door and watched as Mr. Weatherspoon descended the three steps from the porch, past the driver holding the back door open, and entered the grand automobile. The driver hastened to his seat once his master's door was closed, and then pulled smoothly down the curving driveway, past the carefully-designed landscaping, and on to the public road.

CHAPTER EIGHT
Not Hooey
1921

The nanny was uncomfortable standing in the doorway of Mr. Weatherspoon's private office. She looked around the premises and saw him sitting at a huge ornamental mahogany desk. He motioned to one of the two leather chairs set before it, indicating where she should sit.

The room was decorated with clutch pencil sketches of railroad locomotives. To the left was a marshal barrister book case and a file cabinet.

She made her way to her seat. *Such a "male" room, foreboding.*

The smell of sweet pipe tobacco filled the room; his favorite to smoke after a hearty breakfast. Her eyes met Warren's as she sat down. "Thank you for giving me your time, Sir." She adjusted the shirt of her black, high-necked dress. Her shoes practical. She wore no makeup.

My gosh, this woman's proper stiff.

His elbows were placed on the desktop as he leaned forward. One hand held the other, which was holding the pipe bowl.

"Anything to do with Kimberly is important."

"Yes, Sir. I worry for your child's emotional well-being. Love, Sir. I don't think she feels loved."

Surprised, Warren took the pipe from his mouth and sat back in his chair, not expecting candidness.

"I don't understand. The child has everything." He indicated 'everything' with a wave of the hand holding his pipe. "She's provided for very well, don't you think?"

"Yes, Sir, and no, Sir. She enjoys the amenities you provide, but she doesn't feel love. She has everything you have given her, but she needs your attention. She needs you to relate to her,"

A grunt as he placed the pipe in his mouth for a draw. *How to relate to a six-year-old child.*

The nanny watched his body tighten.

"I hire you for her emotional needs."

Sternly. "I cannot be her father."

"You can guide her."

"She's your blood. She needs you."

Warren relaxed his shoulders. "You drive a hard bargain."

"I apologize for being blunt." She softened her approach with a sigh, and a change of pace. "Mr. Weatherspoon, when you conduct your business, don't you start by relating to people first? I don't mean to tell you your business, Sir. I'm simply pointing out that I see a need for you to relate to Kimberly."

"I thought I was doing that."

"No. You ask her if she needs anything, if she wants anything. You ask her if she's happy."

"That's right. What's wrong with that?"

"You need to ask her what's going through her mind. Ask her what she did that day, what she learned at school. Sometimes children sense things we adults do not see. Make a connection with her."

Hmmm. The nerve. Out loud: "Well put, Miss – what's your name? Sorry."

"That's another thing, Mr. Weatherspoon. Nanny's come and go here. She has no consistency with adult females."

"That's because her mother died."

"I know that, Sir. I'm sorry for that. Kimberly, too. But she needs family guidance. It's what a mother would do for Kimberly. Since there is no mother, you are the only one who can give her guidance."

"Alright. Is there anything else?"

"Yes." She straightened her back. "Consider reading her a story at bedtime. Maybe take her to the park on a Sunday afternoon. How about a movie? There's a new one called "*The First Circus*". It's animated."

"What's animated?" he asked.

"Umm, it's characters that have been drawn by an artist and they appear to move."

"Humph," Warren retorted. "Why don't you take her to see that?"

Her shoulders slumped. "Yes, Sir. Only if YOU agree to listen when she tells you about the movie."

He laughed. "You are persistent. I'll consider it. Is there anything else?"

"No, Sir. Thank you, Sir."

"Then have a good day."

She got up from her chair, made her way to the door, paused and turned around before she left.

"My name is Miss Ellen."

Respectfully, she closed the door behind her.

Early morning, not yet dawn, soft and warm in bed. Kimberly stretched her arms above her head, arched her back, flexed her calves and pointed her toes. Not quite awake, but conscious of a new day, she smiled, then dozed.

It was Saturday. No school.

Her thoughts rambled over her homework and friends, particularly Carolyn. Her father a Baptist Minister in Libertyville, fire and brimstone. The girls had similar points of view – propriety in its extreme, using their social status as their exceptional God-given right. Others thought them '*high hat*'.

Kimberly did not stir when she heard a soft knock at the door. Nor did she indicate her awareness when Warren walked into her bedroom and carefully closed the door, making no sound. He approached, past the foot of her bed, then along the opposite side. He lay down on the covers and held her close to him.

She pretended to sleep. He put his face into her hair, detected a lavender scent, Lucinda's favorite. She caught a whiff of her father's favorite pipe tobacco.

Kimberly let her mind wander, accepting caresses in a loving embrace.

CHAPTER NINE
Scholae And Riley
1924

Wearing a sky-blue dress with a dropped waist, her hair falling past her shoulders in banana curls, nine-year-old Kimberly skipped down the winding staircase to join her father for breakfast. She continued skipping, through the tiled entryway and into the dining room, where she took a chair next to Warren on the long end of the table.

"Good morning, Father."

Warren was eating his breakfast of croissants and boiled eggs as he sat facing the entryway.

"There you are. How did you sleep last night, Kimberly?"

"Fine. I kept dreaming about a new pony."

Warren caught a headline in the morning newspaper as Kimberly talked, ignoring her reply.

William served Kimberly her breakfast of orange juice, eggs and croissants. Kimberly hardly noticed him. She grabbed her fork and cut a piece of egg, while reaching for a crystal bowl containing butter and jam.

Warren's focus was interrupted by her zest and he looked at his daughter.

"You *are* hungry!"

Kimberly nodded.

"I need to tell you something."

Kimberly concentrated on her food.

"Pay attention, Kimberly."

She put her fork down, looked at her father, and waited.

"I have enrolled you in a good boarding school."

Kimberly's eye went wide with shock.

"You are growing up and it's time you learned things the local public school can't teach you. I want you to know people in our own station; to learn things, social things."

"But I have friends at school," she interrupted.

Warren's patience was waning. This concerned what her teacher had told him. Kimberly was buying presents for some of her school mates.

"She's buying alliances..." the teacher explained, "...friends...it's making the students uncomfortable. They do not know what to expect from her and they feel obligated to give her something back. It's difficult for them, because they cannot afford what you can afford, Sir."

Warren winced, recalling the teacher's words, though he appreciated the teacher's honesty. He looked sternly at Kimberly. "Good friends will always stay your friends, but you'll also make new friends at the boarding school."

She pouted, sticking out her lower lip. Her breathing turned into a gasping rhythm. "I won't go!"

Warren furrowed his eyebrows, boring his eyes into her. He leaned forward a little bit, suggesting she back off. *She's so obstinate. I don't have time for this. She needs a mother to give her a good spanking.* "That's enough. The decision has been made."

He shifted the morning paper to the front of his face, as if his child was not in the room. A second later, he picked up his fork and continue eating, ignoring her.

Kimberly whined.

He looked up at the butler. "William, please fetch the nanny."

William rushed out of the dining room. *What is her name? Josephine? No that was last week. Ah, yes, Bernice.*

Wearing her servant's uniform, Bernice hurried into the dining room.

"Come along, Kimberly. We'll finish your breakfast in the kitchen."

William pulled back Kimberly's chair as Bernice offered her hand to the barely sniffling girl.

"I'm not a child," she said, mimicking her father's persona. She looked at Warren and the newspaper he used as a wedge between them, then paused as she bit her lower lip.

Pay attention to me! Why do you want me to go away? Useless. You don't like me.

She turned and left the dining room. Warren never knew how he made her feel.

When Kimberly finished breakfast, Bernice tried to help her feel better about the boarding school.

"Let's go upstairs, look through your things and decide what you'll take with you."

"They probably have uniforms," Kimberly said with disdain.

"Even if they do, you won't be wearing a uniform all the time. How about we take a look?"

Kimberly left her chair at the kitchen table and made her way to her bedroom, with Bernice following.

The room had a wispy feeling, wrapped in sheer draping, lace and satin. Morning sunlight shining on a garden below could be seen through the ivory curtains, hung in a crisscross fashion, with lace ruffles gathered at the edges. Two floral-patterned cloth chairs sat in front of the window, with delicate table between them. The single-sized bed, covered with a pink satin quilt, was flush against the wall next to the bedroom door. A canopy, mimicking the curtain lace, stretched over the bed. A chest of drawers and a triple-mirrored dressing table, with a skirt that matched the bed quilt, were arranged on a wall adjacent to the window. To the left was a clothes closet that included a dressing area and bathroom.

Kimberly opened the closet's double doors and searched through her garments.

"Do you think they'll have horses there?" She looked over her shoulder at Bernice.

"No, they don't have horses, but I think you should have play clothes. The school grounds are wooded, so there might be outdoor activities."

"How about this?" Kimberly grabbed a hanger and her eyes glowed with pleasure as she showed Bernice a ruffled dress of emerald green satin with a thick, white lace sash around the waist.

"Oh, how lovely! But it's too formal." Bernice shook her head.

Kimberly frowned. She hung up the dress in the closet and chose another frock.

An hour passed with casual talk about boarding school, what to expect and what to wear.

Part of Bernice's job was to keep Kimberly entertained while under her watchful eye. There were times when Kimberly's need for attention and affirmation exhausted her.

I wonder if this is why she's had so many nannies? Demanding. It's because she's empty inside.

She yawned, releasing tension, while she watched Kimberly chatter on about her clothes, shoes, little hats and purses. "What about jewelry?" Bernice asked.

"Oh yes!" Kimberly hurried over to the triple-mirrored dressing table and opened her jewelry box. Bernice stood behind to observe her mirrored image as Kimberly chose necklaces, bracelets, hair barrettes and pins. She uttered appropriate oooh's and ahhh's, finding ways to engage with Kimberly. The child's flawless facial features, bright golden hair and strikingly white skin made her appear angelic.

The nanny suddenly thought of daffodils, white and gold. "Kimberly, you are one lovely little girl… I mean, young lady."

"Thank you," Kimberly replied, with a beaming smile.

* * *

The night had its own warmth with varying shades of black and shadows created by street lamps, the moon and the stars. Quiet and serene, there was the occasional whisper of voices, sometimes gay, other times gaudy-drunk, with strains of music leaking from local taverns. Few people milled about in the streets.

Riley always found comfort in the shades of night-dark.

He gathered the wool coat collar around his neck to ward off the November chill, as he moved quickly down Raymond Street toward the Elgin National Clock Company Observatory. Riley avoided the bright street lights when he could, their brilliance irritating.

A uniformed night watchman, night stick in hand, walked down the sidewalk across the street. Riley knew him as one of the Elgin Watch Factory security guards. They made eye contact and nodded a mutual gesture of greeting. The night watchman knew Riley, a thin, five-foot-six, albino, with violet eyes and pink lips.

Must be on his way to work.

They heard a trolley car whistle several blocks away. The shrill sound cutting through the cold, breezy night.

Riley looked up at the two-story white building on the corner of Watch and Raymond Streets. The observatory dome was turned around, obscuring the telescope direction. He skipped up the stairs to the entrance.

They probably closed it during the rain storm earlier today.

Riley loved his job and what it made possible. His observations and measurements of the stars acquired the data necessary to allow Elgin time-pieces to be set to an accuracy of one-hundredth of a second.

He unlocked the front door and entered, relocking it from inside. He turned and made his way to the heavy steel door of the observatory area. He fumbled with his keys, found the right one and unlocked the heavy door, relocking it from inside. Then, he started up the winding stairs to the observatory itself.

The observatory contained expensive equipment, so strict security measures protected the highly technical instruments.

Riley entered, then looked around the domed enclosure, assuring that the room had been satisfactorily maintained. After a deep breath and sigh, he began the task of re-positioning a three-foot opening in the sheet-metal-encrusted dome. This process required moving steel shutters, each weighing a ton and a half, with a gearing system so efficient a child could use it.

Once the telescope was set, he began his observations of the stars.

Always a pleasure observing stars and planets. Sometimes a meteor streaked across the night sky, interrupting calculation concentration. They were always welcome events for Riley, looking at the sky of magnificence.

* * *

Several vertical wires cross the eye-piece of the telescope. When a star crosses one of the wires, the astronomer would press a button, sending a signal to two Riefler clocks (precision regulator clocks) that resided in a temperature-controlled vault.

* * *

Having collected data during his allotted time, Riley wrote his observation report for his boss's review.

A night's work done, he could have left the observatory, but he stole a few minutes of telescope time to search the sky for Uranus, whose scheduled appearance was due at three-fifteen in the morning.

At four in the morning, he left the Elgin Watch Factory and headed for his apartment. The trolley cars had just started their scheduled early morning runs.

CHAPTER TEN
Roache Boarding School
1924

The nine-foot-tall stone wall had iron railing on the top. The gate, also iron, was a gothic design, such that each vertical rail spiked. Through the rails one could see forested property. The three-story stone house, obviously built with materials from the same quarry as the property barrier. Foreboding and cold.

The house had many chimneys to ward off the damp chill of Illinois' fall, winter and early spring. The entryway particularly spectacular due to a glass dome hovering over a white-tiled floor, with an Irish family crest outlined in dark brown tile. It represented the pride of the original owner.

Michael Angelo's mural of the hand of God reaching out to the hand of Man was replicated in the glass dome design, with a display of daylight sky and night-time firmament. A third-floor balcony protruded to the edge of the glass dome, so one could better observe the stars. Access to the balcony was not discernable from this vantage point.

Kimberly looked up at the mansion, modified into a girl's boarding school, as she sat in the back of the car. As the automobile neared the front door, the driver honked the horn, announcing their arrival.

A wind gust blew dry leaves all about them. The gray sky threatened a rain shower.

The Head Mistress opened the front door and stepped outside, wrapping her knit shawl closer around her. Her long black skirt protected her legs from the cold.

The driver stopped the car and opened the back door so that little Kimberly could step outside. Then he grabbed suitcases from the trunk and escorted the little girl to the Head Mistress. The lady looked frail, almost anorexic, her light brown hair braided into a bun.

"You must be Miss Oberson."

"Yes, how do you do," she replied, then shivered and wrapped herself more tightly. "This must be Miss Kimberly."

"How do you do," Kimberly replied with a short curtsey.

"Come inside. Let's get you out of the wind."

The driver handed Miss Oberson the suitcases, headed back to the car and got inside. He started the engine just as the females turned and went inside.

The next morning, Kimberly snuggled into the warm sheets of her bed. She knew she had to rise soon, and though still groggy, she reflected on the prior day's events.

Too new, too startling, this boarding school and everything unfamiliar, stark and cold. Miss Oberson seemed alright, easy going and warm, but the rest of the staff, soulless ghosts moving about the building cold.

She opened her eyes and looked about her small room. On top of the chest of drawers, a picture of her father. He was slimmer then and physically adept. Now he was heavier having since taking a liking to bourbon which sometimes flushed his puffy face.

She continued scanning the room. There was a small, mirrored, dressing table where perfume, hairbrushes and hair ribbons lay atop. The skirt of that table matched the cushion top of the stool set before it.

A private bathroom was to the right of the bed and a small nightstand to the left. Just beyond was a window overlooking the wooded school grounds.

Kimberly viewed her surroundings as fundamentally bare, which was not too far from the truth, since this room was once a servant's room.

She got up to urinate, and then scurried back to her warm bed, briefly gazing out the window and noting it was still dark outside. She tucked herself back in bed. A few tears rolled down onto the pillow.

New surroundings, new people, unsettled, no friends. Overwhelming.

She dozed off another hour until she heard a knock on the door.

"Wake up, Miss Kimberly. Breakfast is in one hour."

"Thank you."

Later, she descended two stories, making her way to the dining hall on the main floor. She remembered where it was, having had a tour of the building by Miss Oberson the day before. Entering the dining room, she saw Miss Oberson and five other girls sitting at the dining table.

"Hello, Kimberly. Please join us while we wait for the other students." She pointed to a seat next to a girl about the same age as Kimberly.

Kimberly scanned the faces looking up at her. *I'm prettier than these girls.*

She took her seat.

A few moments passed as the other girls entered the dining hall and sat down. Kimberly scrutinized each young lady as they sat down.

That one is too fat. She has filthy nails. Ugh....

Eventually, all twenty-two young ladies were seated, Miss Oberson began speaking.

"Welcome to Roache Boarding School. This school was founded by the Roache family; whose heritage goes all the way back to the seventeen-hundreds in Ireland. We are very fortunate to have this facility at our disposal for the needs of the very genteel young ladies we have in Libertyville.

You come from admirable origins and so your needs are extraordinary. This is the purpose of this school. Our educational services are designed for the special debutants you are.

While our curriculum includes standard subjects, English, Mathematics, Science, Geography, History, we also provide special classes required by your station in life, including music, dance, architectural design, fashion design, art, etiquette, gourmet cooking, and a study of the classics. These are all the things you will need to make your way through the social expectations of the privileged class of which you have been endowed.

Do not be discouraged by the number of things with which you must become acquainted. It will become easy. We are here to help you achieve your dreams which are to make you young ladies exceptionally suitable for marriage."

She paused.

"Do you have questions?"

A hand raised. A nod in response.

"Why do we have to learn gourmet cooking? Don't we have servants for that?"

"You must learn about spices, their uses and complimentary palates. You also need to know about wines and spirits customary in a fine dining experience."

Eyebrows raised, the girls looked at each other, not knowing what to do or say.

The twelve-year-old sitting next to Kimberly, whispered into her ear.

"Sounds like we are being groomed to be geishas." She giggled.

Kimberly didn't know what a geisha was, but she giggled anyway. Their two heads close together, Kimberly noticed her heart-shaped necklace engraved with the name "Dorothy".

CHAPTER ELEVEN

Pan

1924

Dorothy and Kimberly became fast friends and shared their free time together. An observer of the girls saw the two angelic figures much admired, both having fair skin. Kimberly, at ten years, with blond hair, and Dorothy, at twelve, with strawberry blond hair. They were both petite, feminine in appearance and gesture.

Later that afternoon, the girls were chatting in Dorothy's room, which was exactly like Kimberly's room. She looked into Dorothy's closet. Inquisitive.

Her clothes aren't as nice as mine. Maybe I can help Dorothy with her wardrobe.

She turned her head towards Dorothy and asked, "By the way, what is a geisha?"

"Oh, my father worked for the American Ambassador to Japan, Charles MacVeagh. He told us stories about Japan. Geisha's are women whose purpose is to entertain men. They are well educated, trained in the arts and paid to attend parties."

"Really? Paid to attend parties?"

"Yes. My father didn't tell me too much, but I think it's hilarious."

They both laughed.

"Let me show you. My dad gave me this."

Dorothy went to her nightstand and retrieved a miniature Japanese doll. She then handed it to Kimberly, who examined the doll, fingering the gold silk kimono embroidered with flying gray cranes and a navy obi from just below the navel to the breastbone wrapped around the waist. White socks and sandals added to the authentic Asian image. Jet black hair was geometrically coiffed and her face painted white with tiny red lips. One delicate hand held an unfolded fan in a demure pose.

How different.

Kimberly shook her head. "They wear this at parties?"

"Uh huh…" Dorothy replied. "It's like what we are doing here in school. We are being prepared, too."

Kimberly pushed back a strand of her hair. "Yes, but we don't wear this."

"No but let me show you some of my Vogue magazines – like this one." Dorothy picked out a publication.

She continued, "Look at the large sash, the folds in the cloth and the fan."

Kimberly looked at the image carefully. "I see what you mean. It is like your doll, but different."

Dorothy nodded.

Kimberly scrutinized the picture more carefully, squinting. "What's the picture on the fan?"

Dorothy took the magazine for closer examination. "I don't know. Let's ask Miss Oberson… later."

After dinner, the girls took the magazine to Miss Oberson and asked about the design on the fan, depicting a half-ram, half-human figure reaching out to a scantily-clad woman, who seemed to be running away from him. The outline of her breasts showed through supple red cloth.

Miss Oberson's face flushed red, embarrassed. She looked at the girls, not knowing what to say at first, then having gathered her wits, she adjusted her demeanor.

"That is the Greek god, Pan. Where did you get this?"

Dorothy shrugged her shoulders, "I have several Vogue magazines. I like to read them and look at the pictures. This one is a favorite."

"Well, Vogue is a good fashion magazine."

She handed the magazine back to Dorothy, preserving the children's innocence, since they were not aware of the suggestive message delivered by Pan's lascivious gesture, or the man in the forefront, bent over kissing the lady's hand.

Kimberly had noticed Miss Oberson's shift from embarrassment to a nonchalant attitude.

She's keeping something from us. I wonder what it is...and why?

* * *

All the girls were gathered in the entryway of the grand school, sitting on chairs placed for the girl's talk about astronomy. They chatted among themselves in whispers until Miss Oberson clapped her hands, signaling the start of their lecture.

Next to Miss Oberson was a tall thin man, shuffling his feet, clearly uncomfortable. His white skin pale. Miss Oberson clapped her hands again.

"Ladies, I have the pleasure of introducing to you, Mr. Riley Nacht, who is an astronomer for the Elgin Watch Factory. Let's give Mr. Nacht a nice welcome."

Soft, feminine applause for Mr. Riley Nacht, accepting his unusual appearance – an albino.

"Greetings, ladies. How many of you have watched the stars?" He raised his eyes toward the glass dome, gesturing his hands above his head.

Everyone raised their hand. Satisfied he had gained their attention, he began his lecture.

He talked about how the earth revolves around the sun, about planets and stars, and the astronomical observations he did to set the precision of Elgin watches, using a telescope pointed to the night sky. At length, he noticed he was losing the interest of his audience; a yawn here and there, slouched posture, and crossed arms, so he shifted his talk to Greek mythology and their association with the constellations.

"Her name was Athena, born a full-grown woman out of the head of Zeus, the god of the gods."

A hand raised.

"Yes?"

"How can a woman be born out of a head?"

"Good question." Mr. Nacht paused. "Mythology has metaphorical stories. Consider ideas that produce something tangible. For example, if you sew a dress you must have an idea of the dress beforehand, agreed?"

The girls nodded.

"Zeus had an idea. Being a god, he created his idea in the form of a woman who was intelligent and brave in battle. She shows up in myths represented in the stars."

The girls were now riveted.

"In one story, she watches over the star constellation, Capricorn, where the god, Pan, can be seen."

Dorothy and Kimberly looked at each other in silent connection, recalling Dorothy's picture.

"Pan was a god who liked music, dance and romance. He was smitten by a wood-nymph – think of a fairy – who avoided him by changing herself into a flute. He found the instrument and discovered it rendered doleful music beautifully. Most pictures of Pan show him playing that flute."

A hand raised and Mr. Nacht nodded.

"Why did the flute play sad music?"

"Probably longing, …unfulfilled desire."

Another hand raised. He nodded.

"Did Pan ever marry?"

"No. He wanted to marry a nymph named Echo but she loved Narcissus. Narcissus was very beautiful. One day he admired his reflection on a water surface so intently that he fell in and drowned. After his death, Echo eventually wasted away. She is remembered by sounds made inside of caves and hollow places."

Mr. Nacht then looked at Miss Oberson, indicating his lecture was over.

"If you would like, I can come by some evening, when we have no moonlight, and I can show you the stars more clearly."

He pointed to the balcony that stretched to the edge of the glass dome, high above.

Miss Oberson moved next to Mr. Nacht. "That would be nice, Mr. Nacht. I'll contact you to arrange an evening showing. Thank you very much for your entertaining and informative talk."

She raised her hands and applauded, nodding her head to the girls, who mimicked her applause.

Mr. Nacht bowed slightly and smiled, amused by the polite pitter-patter of dainty fingers patting plump little palms.

CHAPTER TWELVE

Orion

1925

Two weeks later on Sunday, January 26, 1925, during a new moon, Mr. Riley Nacht headed for his scheduled star-gazing experience through the glass dome of Roache Boarding School. It was one-thirty in the morning.

When he arrived, Miss Oberson opened the front door.

"Greetings, Mr. Nacht." She yawned and pulled her shawl more tightly around her in response to the cold night air. "Come in..."

He smiled at her gesture. "Good morning, Miss Oberson."

"How do you manage this late hour?"

"Why it's the middle of a workday for me. Remember, I sleep during the day."

"Of course, you do. How silly of me. I'm not used to being up at this hour. Come with me, please. I'll show you the way."

She walked through the entryway to a foyer. Riley looked around and observed a sitting room to the left and a grand dining room to the right. Beyond the foyer was a large opening with one hall to the left, the other to the right. At the far end was a staircase leading to a second floor.

Miss Oberson motioned toward the hall on the left.

"This hall leads to rooms that we use for classes. At the end of the hall is a grand room that we use for dancing, music and exercise. The right hall leads to private rooms for our staff."

Mr. Nacht nodded. "How nice."

Miss Oberson started up the stairs. Upon reaching the landing she explained, "These rooms are for the students."

Mr. Nacht looked around. The taupe-colored walls were similar to the taupe shade on the multicolored, flowered pattern in the carpet. The light in both halls was muted, so you could make your way without disturbing anyone. White ceiling molding added to the warmth of the building.

"One more flight, Mr. Nacht. The older girls have rooms on the top floor."

When they got to the top floor landing, Mr. Nacht noticed the same décor.

On this floor, however, was a large balcony that reached to the edge of the glass dome high above. The arched balcony entryway had heavy curtains drawn back by a chord, like the balcony seating area in a theater.

Mr. Nacht walked to the balcony edge and looked up at the twinkling stars. He peered at the floor below and observed a distant view of the Roache family coat of arms in dark brown tiles, contrasted with white.

Upper crust, elegant.

"This will work out nicely," he said, turning toward Miss Oberson.

"Wait here, while I get the girls," she said.

A few moments later, she returned with Kimberly, Dorothy and another younger child, Rose. They were all dressed in night robes and slippers.

"These three; nobody else would wake up," explained Miss Oberson.

"That's fine. Hello, ladies. Who noticed the eclipse yesterday morning?"

Kimberly raised her hand. Mr. Nacht nodded to her.

"I woke up early and looked out my window. It was eerie. Everything went dark, and then became light again."

"That's right," he confirmed. "The moon passed over the sun at ten minutes after seven, blocking out the light. This doesn't happen very often. I'm glad you noticed it, Miss Kimberly."

Kimberly felt triumphant and smiled back at him.

"Some say an eclipse prophesizes a significant forthcoming event, but I don't believe that." He wrinkled his nose. "Okay. So, ladies, let me tell you about the stars. Let's turn out the lights, so you can see the sky more clearly."

Miss Oberson left to turn off the lights on the second and third floor. Everything was dark. It took a moment for their eyes to adjust. In the dim starlight, they could barely make each other out.

"When I was here earlier, I mentioned Orion in the stars, but I did not tell you the story in Greek mythology, in Homer's Illiad. Orion was a great hunter, who was begat by the sea-god, Poseidon, and the King of Crete's daughter. As a son of Poseidon, he could walk upon the waves of the sea. He also hunted with the goddess, Artemis. Eventually, he threatened to kill every animal on earth."

"Why?" asked little Rose.

Miss Oberson stifled a chuckle. "It's part of the story, dear. Let's listen."

Riley continued. "Because Orion was a hunter. That's what hunters do. Mother Earth objected to this and sent a giant scorpion to kill him..."

A soft gasp from the girls.

"...and Orion died. In mourning his death, the goddesses appealed to Zeus to place Orion somewhere in the stars. Zeus complied. He also placed the scorpion in the stars, so that others would remember Orion's death." Riley paused briefly. "That ladies, is the constellation, Scorpius."

"Can we see that?"

"No. It's January. Scorpius is only visible in the Northern Hemisphere during July, on hot summer nights."

Rose started to cry quietly. The others ignored her.

"Behold the cosmic display," began Riley, pointing to the sky. "Do you see the bright star that forms the upper torso of Orion? Look at the elongated pentagram. That is Orion's upper torso. The bottom of the pentagram, the three stars, close together, are his belt. Notice that either end of his belt are the beginnings of his legs. Over to the right are stars forming a bent bow. His arms are to the left, high above his head, pulling back the bow-string."

The girls leaned against the balcony rail, arching their necks and straining their eyes.

"I think I see it," said Kimberly.

"Over there," Mrs. Oberson pointed out for Rose.

"Do you mean those stars?" asked Dorothy.

Riley stood behind her to get a closer perspective of what she was seeing.

"No, over there."

Rose was getting dopey with sleep. Miss Oberson felt a slight chill down her spine and tightened her shawl around her shoulders again. "Looks like little Rose needs to go back to bed. Let me turn on the lights for a moment while I take her."

"Sure."

Kimberly spoke up then. "I'll go with you and turn out the lights on my way back."

"Thank you, Kimberly."

They retreated with Rose in tow, the lights on, headed for Rose's room.

Having reached the ground floor, Kimberly watched Miss Oberson carry Rose to her room and enter. She then turned off the ground floor lights and headed back upstairs.

On the second landing, she turned off the lights, then paused when she heard muffled, nearly undetectable sounds. Heading up to the third-floor, she found that the lights had already been turned off. It took a second for her vision to adjust to the darkness.

Reaching the third landing, she hesitated when she again heard the whispered sounds.

She felt a prickly chill down her spine, a warning, so she tiptoed toward Mr. Nacht and Dorothy, then pressed against the wall, inching forward until she was behind the heavy curtain tied against the balcony entryway.

She peered at the barely visible scene before her.

Riley put his right arm around Dorothy's waist and pointed to the glass-domed window with his raised left arm.

"Do you see Orion? Count the window panes to the left."

Whispering. "I think so."

Kimberly deliberately slowed her breath. She could now make out their forms in the star light.

Standing so close to Dorothy, he smelled her skin. Musk. He detected menses. His cheek touched the side of her head, hair so soft, fine. He gently touched some wisps of her hair and tucked them under the pink ribbon that tied back her hair. Her profile in the starlight aroused him. He felt a rush in his groin. His head jerked up, looking around, ensuring he was alone with the young girl.

"Here, let me lift you up."

Circling his hands around her waist, Riley lifted Dorothy up high. The smell of musk became stronger.

Dorothy caught her breath. *Can he really bring me closer?*

Riley felt strange, an electrical buzz in his brain, but without any sharp shock. It was a soft sensation. He looked at her, lifted up, and saw Artemis, the virgin Goddess of the Hunt, daughter of Zeus.

He suddenly tossed her to Orion.

She gasped, feeling a push over the balcony railing. Her eyes and mouth wide open. Topsy-turvy. She tumbled.

In a flash, her broken body shattered on the tiled floor below with barely a thump. She did not make a sound.

Kimberly, dropped the heavy curtain, braced back against the wall, holding her breath. She waited. It was only two or three seconds. To her it seemed an eternity.

Stay quiet; breath shallow; mustn't hear me.

Finally, she heard his steps walk away from the railing, down the hall, down the stairs. She waited longer until sure he was gone, for this was truly a dangerous event. The front door opened and closed. She tip-toed from behind the curtain toward the railing and looked over. There was nothing to see except the faint starlight reflected on the tile floor. She hastened back to her room. No one heard her close her bedroom door and settle into her bed.

I'm safe now.

She looked about her room needing validation that everything within her realm was normal. Finally, she closed her eyes.

Relief. Nothing bad will happen to me. I'm special. Perfect. Father is powerful and so am I. No one can hurt me. And I'm beautiful. No one can compete with me. I live in a grand mansion. No one here has a mansion like I do. I have expensive jewelry. Exquisite. Oh, the covers feel so soft and warm. Tomorrow I think I'll wear my new dress. Maybe part my hair to the side with curls....

Comforted, Kimberly slept soundly.

After placing Dorothy's body in the back seat of his automobile, conveniently parked near the front door, Riley entered his car quickly and silently. Nobody heard a car engine rev-up, then drive away through the open iron gates held by two stone pillars of the Roache Boarding School property.

It has been said some killers find eroticism in the hunt; others in the kill. In this case, Riley thought of himself as Orion with Artemis.

I kill because I can.

* * *

When Rose finally went to sleep, Miss Oberson stole away and hastened up the stairs to the third-floor balcony. Everyone was gone.

Shrugging her shoulders, she scurried to the ground floor and bolted the front door. She did not notice a small drop of blood on a brown tile that was part of the entryway floor. The night slippers she wore were knitted so tight that the tell-tale evidence was wiped clean by her hurrying footfalls, heading for bed.

CHAPTER THIRTEEN

Cessatum

1925

The sun had already risen a few hours, Sunday morning, when Dorothy was noticed missing at breakfast. Miss Oberson looked everywhere for the child and when she could not find her, she knew she had to call the police.

Careful. These children must be protected from information while we figure this out. It's possible Dorothy may have run away. Kimberly is friends with her. I'll ask Kimberly.

After she called the police, she found Kimberly in the dining room and asked her to speak with her in her office. Kimberly did as Miss Oberson asked, even though she no longer trusted the woman.

She let Mr. Nacht into the school. What happened to Dorothy was her fault.

"Kimberly, I'm looking for Dorothy. Do you know where she could be?"

"No."

"What happened when you left Rose and I last night?"

"Nothing."

"Did you go back to the balcony?"

"Yes."

"Was there anyone there?"

"No."

"Did you go back to bed?"

"Yes."

"Don't be afraid, child. It's okay to tell me if you saw something."

"I didn't see anything."

Miss Oberson paused, not sure.

"Alright," Miss Oberson replied. "You may go now."

She didn't want to upset the girls, so at breakfast she announced Dorothy had gone and was expected back in about a week.

Kimberly took this news stoically.

I'll never trust Miss Oberson.

An hour later, Miss Oberson showed Chief Sonne into her office for a private chat. She began talking as soon as she closed her office door.

"I don't know what to do, Chief." Wringing her hands, she was clearly distraught. "I can't find Dorothy. I've looked everywhere."

The Chief looked into her bloodshot eyes, dark circles underneath. Her disheveled hair reflected her anxiety.

"When was the last time you saw her?"

"Last night, about one-thirty in the morning." She then explained last night's star gazing event, as the Chief of Police took notes.

"Do you think the child ran away?"

"I don't think so. Dorothy seemed a well-adjusted girl. We screen our students carefully. They come from exceptional families."

"Alright. Let's assume it's *not* a runaway situation. I'll investigate it as such."

Miss Oberson began to quietly weep, then moved from behind her desk to sit next to the Chief. He waited for her to collect herself, a gesture of empathy for her grief, watching as she retrieved a handkerchief from her skirt pocket and sobbed unashamed.

"Oh, God! What if she's dead? I let Mr. Nacht into our school!"

"Don't let your thoughts go to dark places, Miss, we don't know that's the case yet." He paused, then asked, "So, why did you invite him?"

Miss Oberson gulped back a sob. "Mr. Nacht knows astronomy. We try to have different lecturers from different disciplines visit our school as part of expanding the girl's education."

"Have you invited Mr. Nacht before?"

"No. The idea came to me when I bought an Elgin-made wrist watch. I noticed the dome at the Elgin Observatory. I spoke with his management for permission. I thought I was careful. After all, Elgin Watch Factory is a reputable institution."

"Yes, it is," he said reassuringly.

"Should I call her parents? They'll ask me questions I can't answer."

He considered her thought. *If this is nothing, then we've alarmed her parents for no reason and we've alarmed the community. It's unlikely there's a criminal act here.*

"Give me some time to look into this – today and tomorrow. She may show up. Meanwhile, I'll have Deputy Phillips search the school premises today."

"Can you do that at lunch time when everyone's in the dining room? I don't want the girls alarmed any further."

"Yes...and give me a call if anything else comes up."

"Alright. Waiting will be agonizing. Please let me know if you find anything."

"I will. I promise."

Chief Sonne walked outside toward his car.

I can't believe this is happening. If the worst did occur, it'll be the first in my career.

He entered his vehicle, donned his reading glasses and perused his notes. Then he looked off into the distance to think while holding his glasses in his hand.

Star gazing? Really? Unusual. The little girl. What's her name?

Donning his eyeglasses again, he glanced at his notes.

Kimberly Weatherspoon. Hmmm, ah yes, Mr. Warren Weatherspoon, of course, so this is HIS daughter. No help. She didn't see or hear anything. No clue what had happened. Poor Miss Oberson.

He placed the key into the ignition and started the engine.

Child abduction, no small thing. I hope she's still alive.

Down the driveway through the open property gates, he decided his next task.

First, get his address and talk to Mr. Riley Nacht.

* * *

Riley had been asleep for three hours when he heard a thundering knock on the front door of his apartment.

"Police! Open the door!"

Sleepily, he put on his slippers and robe, tightening the sash and shuffled to the door, opening it before the pounding could resume.

"Are you Mr. Riley Nacht?"

Yawning, Riley nodded his head.

"We'd like to ask you a few questions, Sir."

"What's this about?"

"I am conducting an investigation. I'd like to ask you a few questions."

"Come in. Sit down." Riley gestured to a chair near a couch set against a wall. He took the couch.

The Police Chief noticed the darkness of the apartment and the heavily curtained windows.

It all seemed so explainable. A man who works all night. A lecture given in the middle of the night, which accounted for his presence. That Miss Oberson and little Rose left the star gazing session and were gone for a while. The lecture completed. Kimberly and Dorothy went back to bed. He left the boarding school. Nothing unusual.

"Where did you go?" asked the Chief.

"Back to work."

"Is there anyone who can corroborate your whereabouts?"

"No one saw me, but the information I gathered has a date and time noted."

"Fine. That'll work. Thank you, Mr. Nacht. Sorry to have disturbed you."

"You're welcome."

He rose from the couch, showed the Chief to the door and shuffled back to bed.

That was easy. I'd like to go back there. Roache Boarding School - a menu of little girls. That blond one with the white skin. Perfect features. A real beauty with arrogance. Kim-something. She's special....

Riley let his mind scheme before sleep overtook him. A lock of strawberry blond hair, wrapped in pink ribbon, was held next to his heart by hands posed in prayer.

* * *

That evening, Police Chief Sonne sat in his home at the kitchen table, again, perusing his notes. He fiddled with his papers.

*Ah. My interview with Miss Oberson. She left Dorothy with Mr. Nacht to take Rose back to bed. Kimberly tagged along. That left Mr. Nacht **alone** with Dorothy. But Kimberly returned to the balcony, right? I think I'll phone Miss Oberson.*

He called the Roache Boarding School and asked to speak with her. It was a two-minute wait.

"This is Miss Oberson."

"Sorry to interrupt. This is Police Chief Sonne. Would you answer a quick question?"

"Certainly."

"Kimberly was with you and Rose when you put Rose back to bed, right?"

"That's correct."

"Did she stay with you?"

"No. Once we got to Rose's room, Kimberly returned to the balcony, turning off the lights on her way."

"Why did she do that?"

"So that the lights would not compete with the starlight."

"Ah. Did she see anything?"

"I asked her that. The child told me, no. She went back to bed."

"Why did she go back to bed?"

"Because there wasn't anyone there."

"Thank you, Miss Oberson."

"You're welcome."

He looked at his notes again.

Mr. Nacht said Dorothy and Kimberly went back to bed at the same time. I wonder who is lying.

He decided to take a shower before going to bed. Relax his muscles. He let the water stream down his back as he leaned into the shower wall.

Nacht is lying. Not Kimberly. Nacht has an obvious motive if he's a killer.

Towel-drying himself, he considered the flip-side – Kimberly lying.

If Kimberly lied, that means she saw something – she saw Nacht with Dorothy. Nah. I can't believe that. She's just a kid. Why would she collude with Nacht?

He donned his pajamas and slid into bed, hoping for a good night's sleep. Jolted by a thought, he sat up.

Because she was afraid!

CHAPTER FOURTEEN
Investigation
1925

Chief Sonne woke early Monday morning. He couldn't eat breakfast, couldn't stomach it yet, too wrapped up in this mystery. Instead, he drank a cup of coffee, heavy on the cream and sugar. He retrieved pencil and paper, from a kitchen drawer and began to jot down the day's itinerary. Nervous energy soon pushed him to alternately dress and write, hurrying between his bedroom and the kitchen.

I only have one deputy. I wonder if I should call Horace McMann? He promised to be a reserve officer, if needed. Nah, not yet. Need to get more information first.

Half-dressed he walked to the kitchen for another cup of coffee.

Might have to call the Chicago Superintendent for help. It's possible this situation needs trained and experienced officers. I'm pretty sure he'll oblige.

First, call Deputy Sherman Phillips. Then, call Miss Oberson to arrange an interview with the child. After that, maybe call Chicago. Might be prudent to call Horace McMann after all. Tell him he may be needed to back up Deputy Phillips if something happens here. Need to verify Mr. Nacht's whereabouts last night, see if I need to interview him again.

He looked at his Elgin-made wrist watch. Seven o'clock. He called his deputy.

"Sorry to wake you, Sherm."

"That's okay. What's up?"

"When you went through Roache Boarding School yesterday, did you find anything?"

The Chief heard him yawn. "Not a thing, Chief. If I had found something, I would have called you. You know that. What's going on?"

"I'm not sure yet. Still trying to piece it together. I'm operating on a worse case perspective, just to be prepared. I need you to take over headquarters while I do some more investigating today. Maybe tomorrow, too."

"Okay."

"I'll give Horace a call to put him on stand-by if you need police assistance while I'm busy."

"That bad, huh?"

"Could be, Sherm. I'm being careful. I'd like you to be alert too, alright? Just keep your eyes and ears open."

"Yes, Sir. I'll let you know if anything unusual happens on this end."

"Thanks, Sherm."

Next, the Chief prepared himself for his call to Miss Oberson.

Betcha she's at her desk. Probably didn't sleep last night.

He guessed right.

"Roache Boarding School, Miss Oberson speaking."

"Hello, this is Chief Sonne."

"Good to hear from you."

"Did you get any sleep last night?"

"Heavens no," she replied.

"I'm sorry about that. I hope to get to the bottom of this soon."

"I appreciate that, Chief."

"So, I need to talk to Kimberly Weatherspoon. When is a good time for me to stop by?"

"Of course. The girls are having breakfast now. Why don't you come between eight and eight-thirty?

"Fine. I'll be there in about thirty minutes."

"Um, Chief Sonne, I'd like to be there when you talk to her. Keep in mind, the child is only ten-years-old. She may not be responsive to you. She might be intimidated. I'm very protective about my girls."

"Absolutely."

* * *

Thirty minutes later, Miss Oberson and Kimberly were waiting in the Head Mistress's office when the Chief arrived. He knocked on the office door.

"Come in, Chief Sonne," Miss Oberson said.

When he opened the door, he saw Miss Oberson sitting at her desk, wearing a black dress. Kimberly was sitting in a chair situated in front of the desk.

There's stress on her face, circles under her eyes.

"You saw me come in through the window, huh?" he smiled at her, gesturing toward the office window with a view of the front garden.

"Yes, we did." Miss Oberson smiled back. She understood he was attempting to soften the tone of the meeting.

"Let me introduce you to Miss Kimberly Luc Weatherspoon. Kimberly, this is Police Chief Sonne."

Kimberly, impeccably dressed, wore a lilac dress with a dropped waist and three-quarter length sleeves. Her hair was parted to the side with curls held back by jeweled pins. Her white stockings complemented her black patent leather shoes. She wore a gold necklace that held a pearl pendant. He walked to her and offered his hand.

"How do you do?"

Kimberly looked at Sonne, considered his uniform and his police badge. *Daunting.* Her hand-shake limp.

The Chief saw her hesitancy. "Luc is an unusual name. Where does it come from?"

"My mother's name was Lucinda. My father called her Luc."

The Chief noticed Kimberly referred to her mother in past tense. He decided to stay away from a bad subject.

Miss Oberson gestured to the chair next to Kimberly. "Please, have a seat, Chief."

"Thank you." Then looking at the little girl, he asked. "May I call you Kimberly?"

"Yes."

The Chief's first impression of Kimberly intrigued him.

Very unusual. Superior attitude.

"How do you like it here at school, Kimberly?"

Kimberly looked at Miss Oberson, and then at the Police Chief. *I wonder why he's asking me this?* "It's all right, I suppose."

"You must be wondering why I'm here. I'm looking for Dorothy. Do you have any idea where she may be?"

"No."

"Will you please tell me when you last saw her?"

"We were star gazing at night with Mr. Nacht, an astronomer."

"That was on the third-floor balcony, looking through the glass dome, right?"

"Yes," Kimberly closed her hands together on her lap. Her right thumb rubbing the knuckle of her left index finger. *He knows more than he's letting on.*

"Who was with you, besides Mr. Nacht?"

"Miss Oberson, Rose and Dorothy."

"There was a moment when you went with Miss Oberson and Rose to put Rose to bed, right?"

Kimberly's expression changed, her face concerned, eye's watering. The adults saw her harden. "Yes."

"What happened when you returned to the balcony?"

Her eye brows furrowed, teeth clenched. The adults noticed her breathing shifted to panting. Miss Oberson became alarmed. "It's all right, Kimberly. Tell the officer the truth."

Kimberly started to cry. "I DON'T know where Dorothy is, alright? Why are you asking me? I don't know!"

Miss Oberson left her chair and hurried to Kimberly, kneeling before her, embracing. Kimberly pressed her face into Miss Oberson's shoulder, clinging.

"It's alright, child," she tried to reassure her. "The police are trying to understand what happened, that's all."

"I'm NOT a child," she snapped back. "You're trying to make this my fault!"

"Oh no, Kimberly! That's not what's happening. Not at all. We're just trying to understand."

Kimberly wanted to burst out the words, *"It all YOUR fault! You brought Mr. Nacht here!"* But she was too afraid.

She IS trying to make it my fault.

Miss Oberson, her tired face relenting to Kimberly's outburst, said, "Chief, I think you better leave us."

"Yes, of course," he replied. Then, added, "I'm sorry, Miss Kimberly. Please be assured I don't see anything that you did as 'wrong'. I'm just trying to understand what had happened." He waited to see how she would respond.

Nothing.

His tried one more thing. "Did Dorothy run away?"

Kimberly looked up at him for a moment, shook her head, then hid her face again.

The Police Chief left the office, gently closing the door.

Kimberly saw something, I'm sure of it.

He glanced up at the glass dome high above, pausing before he exited the building.

It took maybe five minutes to go to Rose's room and return. Plenty of time for Mr. Nacht to abscond with Dorothy. I wonder why Dorothy didn't fight back or scream? Why was it so quiet? Hmm. Because she was probably incapacitated. Oh my God. I hope she wasn't already dead.

He drove to his office knowing Deputy Phillips was already there. Chief Sonne entered the brick building, ignoring the bold signage:

LIVERTYVILLE POLICE HEADQUARTERS

Deputy Sherm Phillips had never seen Chief Sonne like this before – anxious. Rather than push his boss into an explanation, he walked to the water tank, filled a glass and offered it to Sonne.

"Thanks."

The Chief walked to his desk, grabbed the phone and dialed.

"Howdy, Horace. How are things at the store?"

Horace's grocery store was a three-storied Victorian building, part of the row-house/store architecture typical of the town.

"Fine. Nothing new. Rumor has it something fishy happened at Roache. Is that why you're calling?"

Damn. Can't keep folks from rumor.

"Yeah, I'm looking into it. Can you step in as reserve for Sherm if something happens?"

"How long will you need me?"

"Figure one or two days, max."

"Sure. My son will take over the store. What's going on?"

"Can't tell you right now."

"That bad, huh?"

"Maybe."

"Well, it's gotta be more exciting than what I have going on over here." He looked at his son stacking tomatoes on the store display.

"How'd you find out about Roache?"

"The school cook came by this morning and bought some groceries."

Figures.

"Well, I'd appreciate it if you keep quiet about this."

"Sure, no problem."

"Thanks, Horace."

Click.

He turned to his deputy. "I should be back in a couple of hours."

The Chief drove from Libertyville to the corner of Watch and Raymond Streets in Elgin. The observatory was an obvious building due to the dome on one side.

This is where Mr. Nacht works. Wonder if somebody's in?

He found a parking spot nearby, skipped up some stairs to the building and knocked on the door. No one responded. He checked the door – locked.

He went back to his car and drove around the Elgin Watch Factory estate until he found what looked like to be the main building.

Take a chance here.

He parked his car and walked inside. There was a receptionist at the front desk. She raised her eyebrows when she saw his badge - Libertyville Police Chief Sonne. She was very accommodating. He soon found himself talking to the manager of the Engineering and Science Department.

"Thank you for your time. I need to verify the whereabouts of Mr. Riley Nacht on Sunday morning, January 26."

"Certainly. Let me check my records. It'll take me several minutes."

"That's fine. I'll wait."

Minutes later. "It looks like he arrived to work at nine o'clock Saturday evening and he left at four-thirty Sunday morning."

"Is that usual?"

"Yes. Why do you ask?"

"Because he was at Roache Boarding School that evening."

"Is that so?"

"You didn't know?"

"Well, I guess I did know, now that I recall. I gave him permission to give a lecture there. We sometimes do curtesy events to promote our business."

"Well, I need to verify his whereabouts that evening."

"Why, is there a problem?"

"I don't know yet. He told me after he left Roache, he returned to work. He noted some observations. I understand his notes have a date and time stamp on them."

"Yes. That's our practice."

"May I see these notes?"

The manager, irritated, became snippy. "Is it **that** important, Officer?"

Chief Sonne restrained himself. "I appreciate how inconvenient this must be for you. After all, you must have a busy day with everything precisely scheduled. Police work, Sir, is spontaneous. Our disciplines are different."

The manager laughed. "Quite so. Nicely put. I'll have my assistant, Mr. Langford, take you to the observatory and collect the notes so that you can look at them. Know our business does appreciate the services of law enforcement."

* * *

An hour later, Mr. Langford and Sonne were standing in a ground-floor office of the observatory building, looking through chart notes written early Sunday morning.

"Here's what you're looking for..." Mr. Langford pointed at entries in the log. Looking over his shoulder, Chief Sonne read the notes regarding constellations, latitude, longitude, magnitude, date, time and signature. They were signed RSN.

"RSN?" The Chief raised his eyebrows at Mr. Langford.

"Riley Stan Nacht."

"Is this his handwriting?"

Mr. Langford nodded.

"Do you mind showing me the observatory?"

"Not at all." Mr. Langford closed the log book and put it away. "It is the jewel of our business; extraordinarily magnificent." He beamed. "Follow me. Notice we take special security precautions to protect it."

"I'm sure you do! Is this building always locked?"

"Yes, of course!"

The men made their way to a heavy steel door. Mr. Langford fumbled with his keys, found the right one and unlocked it, relocking it from inside.

The Chief noticed his key fumbling. "How many people have keys to the dome?"

"Five."

"Including, Mr. Nacht?"

"Of course. Everyone who works in this building has a key."

They started up the ornate, spiral iron stairs that led to the observatory itself. Mr. Langford kept his eyes on the top landing as he briskly climbed the staircase.

"There are several vertical wires that cross the eye-piece of the telescope. When a star or a planet crosses one of the wires, the astronomer presses a button to send a signal. The signal is received by special precision regulator clocks for the date and time stamp."

Chief Sonne listened to Langford as he moved slowly up the stairs, carefully observing everything. The distance between the two men increased. He momentarily paused and nearly gasped when he bent over a small object tucked in a stair crevice.

It was a lock of blond hair wrapped in pink ribbon. He quickly snatched it up and carefully put it in his pocket.

Having reached the top landing, Mr. Lanford turned and looked down at him. "Are you okay?"

"Oh, yes," the Chief reassured him, and hurried up the stairs.

CHAPTER FIFTEEN
Emily Of New Moon
1925

Twelve hours later, the groundskeeper, whose habit was to open the property gates before dawn, found Dorothy's head skewered on one of the iron spokes of the front gate. He came upon the gruesome scene by flashlight, his shaking hand creating trembling shadows. Terrified, he ran to the building, into Miss Oberson's office, and called the police. Then he hastened to Miss Oberson's bedroom door and knocked loudly to waken her. Startled, she opened the door and gasped when he told her what had happened.

Indiscreet. Others heard the news.

Miss Oberson quickly dressed and ran to the gate. The same time the police arrived.

Oh, my God! The poor child! Oh, my God! What will her parents think? How do I tell them?

Rumors flew like wildfire throughout the school. It pushed Miss Oberson's professional ability to the limit just to stay calm and thoughtful. She decided to have Police Chief Sonne with her when she called Dorothy's parents to tell them what had happened. Something about a male voice of authority helped convey the terrible news and answer questions.

Chief Sonne, also made the helpful suggestion to call the Theological School located at Elgin State Mental Hospital. Having a priest on the Roache school premises during this difficult time would have a calming effect on everyone.

It was time for her to make an announcement to her students.

She called the girls to gather in the dining room. The whispers already flourished with a hodgepodge of misinformation, as Miss Oberson shushed them down. She scanned the faces of her adolescent audience and settled upon the face of a fifteen-year-old girl, white as a sheet.

"Now, girls, we are all safe. There is nothing to be afraid of. We will stay close together while the police do their job."

She looked behind her, acknowledging the Police Chief, who stood a few feet away. An Episcopal Priest stood next to the officer, starched white collar blazing.

"You probably already know Dorothy is not with us anymore."

Muffled sounds of children weeping softly.

"We can talk about this. I've brought Reverend Chandler to speak. He comes to us from the Theological School at Elgin State Mental Hospital where people are sick and sometimes die. He is well versed in the life experience and what happens when people pass from this earth.

You can call your parents, one at a time, this afternoon. We will leave it up to them if you should stay with us or if you should go home. Either way is fine with us. Should you stay here, we will stay close, so you will not have to worry."

When this is over, and it will be over soon, we will start where we left off. The living continues living life fully. It's God's will that we go forward in our life endeavors, as He sees fit."

* * *

Ring. Ring.

Warren, eating his breakfast in his home office, waited for the butler to answer and screen the call. Normally he would be at his Libertyville office, but today he planned a business trip to Vermont for an important meeting. Seconds passed. A knock on the door.

"Come in."

"Sir, it's Roache Boarding School. It's important."

William handed the phone receiver to Mr. Weatherspoon. "There's been an incident."

Their eyes met with concern as Warren took the receiver. "Hello?"

"Hello, Mr. Weatherspoon. This is Police Chief Sonne. There has been an incident. Your daughter is fine, but a student has been killed. Discovery of this deed was particularly gruesome. The children have been protected from the details of this heinous act and discovery of her body, but rumors are being passed around. We are moving as quickly as possible, informing parents. You are the first one notified."

Now riveted, Warren demanded, "Details."

The Chief coughed. "The little girl's name is Dorothy. She was abducted during the night less than two days ago. Her head was later found on the spikes of the school's entrance gate." A pause. "We're still investigating, so I can't tell you anything more."

"How was she abducted?"

"I'm sorry, I can't say right now. It's important for you to know that Dorothy and your daughter were friends."

Warren grimaced with the weight of this news; right in the middle of a business deal with Dr. Webb, who married into the privileged, Vanderbilt, American-royal line.

Inconvenient. How to handle.

"May I speak with Miss Oberson, please?"

"Of course."

"Hello, Mr. Weatherspoon." Rivulets of perspiration appeared on her face, the strain of it all.

"Hello, Miss Oberson, I hear you have been dealing with quite an ordeal."

She sighed. *Unexpected empathy. Momentary relief.* "Yes, Sir. We feel terrible about this. I have Police Chief Sonne and an Episcopalian priest to help us deal with this tragedy, Sir."

Warren detected the quiver in her voice. She continued. "The priest is from Elgin Mental Hospital and has experience in dealing with catastrophe."

"How is my daughter?"

"She appears fine. I am concerned about her and all our children's emotional well-being, as well as their spiritual well-being."

Warren, slightly annoyed. "How are you going to respond to the children's needs?"

"Talking about it frankly. We'll discuss death from the Christian point of view. I'm also arranging for a psychologist to be involved."

Warren considered the options. *Bring her home? Let her stay?* "It sounds like classes will be interrupted."

"Yes, that's right," Miss Oberson said.

"How long will that last?"

"A few days – three."

"I'd rather Kimberly come home for those three days. I'll send my driver to pick her up as soon as possible."

"As you wish."

Miss Oberson hung up the phone and made her way to the priest.

"Father Chandler, Mr. Weatherspoon doesn't want his daughter, Kimberly, to stay here during this period of grief and reflection. He is sending a car to take her home."

"What? That's not right. Do you mind if I call the man and have a chat with him?"

"No, of course not."

Moments later, the priest had Mr. Weatherspoon on the phone.

"Hello, Mr. Weatherspoon. I want to talk to you about Kimberly's welfare and the recent horrendous event that the children have had to deal with. May I take a few minutes of your time, Sir?"

"Yes, of course."

"Sir, when a tragedy occurs, it's imperative the children express their feelings with each other. It's a confirmation of what had happened. They need to hear their feelings are normal. And then we discuss how to address feelings. It's about emotional stability, Sir. I was told you want to bring Kimberly home. I thought if I explained to you our handling of this delicate situation, you may want to reconsider. I'm sure you are concerned with the welfare of your daughter."

"Yes, she is my highest priority."

"Well then, after we discuss these things, we will talk about how to respond to the loss of the poor child, Dorothy. I will read some Bible verses and we'll pray. It's about closure and how our Divine power can help us. Then, we turn Dorothy's soul to the care of God."

"Well, Father Chandler, you see I don't believe in God. Never did. While your approach may be satisfactory for the other children in this boarding school, the Weatherspoon's have our own way to address this unfortunate event. My decision to bring Kimberly home stands."

Father Chandler winced at Warren Weatherspoon's implication: *Butt out.*

"As you wish. Thank you for your time."

* * *

That afternoon, Kimberly walked through the door of the Weatherspoon mansion. Suitcases were not needed. Plenty of clothes in her room. William greeted her at the door and noticed she was carrying a book with her.

"Welcome home, Miss Kimberly."

He helped her take off her coat. Kimberly wore an expensive navy angora sweater with her dress.

She always looks so pretty. Flawless. "Your father is expecting you in his office."

"Thank you, William." She nodded, held her book close to her chest and started for the hallway.

A gentle knock. "Come in, Kimberly. I've been expecting you."

"Hello, Father."

"Kimberly, sit down, please." He motioned toward one of two leather chairs set in front of his large mahogany desk. Papers were stacked on the desk top. A briefcase on the floor, leaned against the desk side.

"How are you?" He looked at Kimberly closely.

"Fine."

Tenderly, Warren asked. "Please, tell me what happened, child."

"I'm not a child."

Warren sighed. "Oh, yes. I forgot. So, tell me what happened at school."

"Dorothy died."

"Was she a friend of yours?" Warren became concerned.

Kimberly's voice became soft. "Yes. We liked the same things."

"What things? Tell me."

"We talked about clothes and jewelry. She had some Vogue magazines we looked through. Sometimes we were in the same class."

"That's nice. How did she pass away?" Warren was riveted now.

Kimberly leaned against the chair back and shrugged her shoulders while she maintained eye contact with Warren. She still held the book close to her chest.

I wonder what she's thinking. Probably nothing.

He decided to give her direction. "Kimberly, you are growing up quickly. You are not a child anymore."

He watched her reaction and decided to ignore her dismissive eye gesture. He moved the papers around on the top of his desk, then regained eye contact with his daughter.

"The Weatherspoon line is made of hearty stock. We persevere. We don't let on our feelings. Death is a part of life. It's something we must accept. I was there when your mother died, but no one saw me sad, even though I felt that way. I maintained decorum."

He saw her perplexed expression. "Decorum. We maintain our behavior as expected of people in our station of life. If you want to cry, cry in privacy. That is why I brought you home. Do you want to cry?"

Her voice became soft again. "I don't know."

Warren continued. "Well… if you feel that way, use the privacy of your room. Now, I have to travel to Vermont on business later today. I have asked my secretary, Lucy, to take you into Chicago tomorrow on a shopping spree. You'll have lunch there, too. William will come along to help you with packages. Would you like that?"

Kimberly nodded. "Yes, Father."

"You'll go back to school the day after tomorrow."

"Yes, Father."

He considered the object Kimberly was embracing. "What's that I see you holding?"

"It's a book."

"May I see it?"

She handed him the novel.

"Where did you get this?" he asked.

"It was Dorothy's. She lent it to me."

Hmmm. Emily of New Moon by L.M. Montgomery.

He considered his daughter tenderly as he handed the book back to her.

"I think it's okay if you want to keep it."

CHAPTER SIXTEEN
The Police Chief
1925

A shock wave hit the Libertyville community when news of a child's severed head being placed on an iron spike of the Roache Boarding School gate. It ran rampant throughout Libertyville, into Chicago, and to the desk of the Chicago Superintendent of Police.

Ring. Ring.

"This is Police Chief Sonne."

"Hello, Chief. This is Superintendent Collins from Chicago. I heard about the incident at the Roache Boarding School and I want to offer my services should you need support."

"That's mighty kind of you, Sir. In fact, I had intended to call you myself. Glad you beat me to it."

The Superintendent laughed. "We think alike, then." He paused. "Chief, I respect your territory and appreciate your circumstances. If you're like Chicago, your officers are busy with local crime, accidents, drunks and robberies. That's the trend right now. If you need additional support, we'd be happy to serve for a couple of days. It sounds like you have real psychopath on your hands."

"Yeah, well, my jurisdiction is small compared to Chicago. Most folks here are law abiding. They know each other. I have a Deputy and a Reserve Deputy, who is on call. That's it."

"Actually, that sounds kind of nice," Collins chuckled.

"In a lot of ways, it is. I admit I don't have experience with crazies. We do have an insane asylum close by. They are equipped to handle extreme cases, but I've never hunted one down before."

Superintendent Collins breathed a sigh of relief. *Thank God, he's not egotistical. Most men would try to be a hero and end up doing something stupid. This guy is using his head.*

"We have some experience with psychopaths in Chicago. Why don't you take the train to our police station where we can have a chat?"

"Will tomorrow do?" Sonne asked.

"Absolutely. I'll make time for you."

"Thank you, Sir. I'll be there in the morning."

* * *

The next morning, the Chief caught an early train to Chicago for his meeting with Superintendent Collins.

Over coffee in Collins's office, Chief Sonne told the Superintendent about the star gazing event at Roache, and his investigation afterwards. He deliberately left out the evidence he found at the observatory, wanting to see first what the Superintendent would say.

"I don't know much about psychopaths, but this is over-the-top."

"It's about power," the Superintendent told him. "The grisliest criminals are often psychopaths."

Sonne stretched his neck, putting his finger under his shirt collar to adjust it. His clean-shaven neck splotchy with red prickly blemishes bothering him. "Too much starch." He straightened his dark blue top coat, and then sat back in his chair.

Superintendent Collins asked, "Have there been any other Libertyville incidents like this?"

"Possibly. Last year in October and November. The October incident was an eight-year-old female name Lilly-Belle Blake. Reported missing, she has never been found. Then, in November, there was another child missing, Wilma Sacks, seven-years-old. We found her body, but not her head."

"So, let's assume it's one person, probably male. This criminal is escalating…" Collins tapped the arms of his chair. "What happened after that?"

"The Sacks family blamed a cousin and the young man fled west. I put a warrant out for his arrest, but nothing has come up." The Police Chief paused, thinking about the previous crimes while taking a sip of his coffee. He shared his thoughts.

"Yeah, he must be a psychopath. Well, that doesn't leave too many suspects. Dorothy was last seen alive at the boarding school. There is only one live-in man on the premises, the grounds keeper, and he was out of town that night. The only man there about the time of Dorothy's disappearance was Mr. Riley Nacht. He's my main suspect."

Collins leaned forward, listening and nodding. "You had no reason for suspicion when you interviewed him after the child was reported missing. How about you have a talk with him again, but this time, rattle him up a bit and see what comes out? Look for inconsistencies in his story. Also, impulsiveness. This man takes risks, so be alert. He might come at you. Better yet, take some of our police officers for a couple of days. Take him to your police station. When you have him in your custody, my officers will take a look through his apartment. I'll get the judge to sign a search warrant this morning."

"Good idea. I'll bring him to my office tomorrow. The extra help will be appreciated." The Chief extended his hand to the Superintendent. "I can't thank you enough, Sir."

"Everyone benefits, Chief. My police officers get experience, and you, Sir, get to save Libertyville from a dangerous madman."

* * *

Bedded down for the day, Riley was again awakened by banging on his apartment door. He shuffled out of bed, put on his robe and opened the front door. It was Police Chief Sonne, dressed in his navy-blue uniform and white shirt.

"Sorry to wake you, Mr. Nacht. We'd like to take you to police headquarters and ask you a few questions."

"Now?"

"Yes, I'll wait here while you get dressed."

"Is this really necessary?"

"Yes, it is. We also have a search warrant for your apartment."

"What! No. You can't search my home."

The Chief stepped inside the doorway, pushing Riley back. He had to balance tenacity with patience; to provoke his main suspect, without going too far. He remembered the Superintendent's warning. *Psychopaths can be impulsively dangerous.*

Holding the search warrant in front of Riley's face, the Chief said, "This paper says I can. Now, let's go into your bedroom and get you dressed."

Riley looked worried and raked his fingernails through his white hair. He saw at least three police officers standing in the hall behind the Chief.

There has to be a way to avoid this. "I have to go to the bathroom."

"Then go." The Police Chief could see the bathroom at the end of the hall, straight ahead, he noticed a window.

Riley walked through the living room, past a small kitchen, and through the hall leading to the latrine. Chief Sonne nodded to one of the police officers, indicating he should position himself below the window. The officer understood his task.

A few minutes passed, a flush of the toilet, and then Riley opened the bathroom door.

"I'll help you get dressed," said the Chief Sonne, knowing Riley saw the cop below his window. He didn't want to take the chance of losing sight of Riley.

It didn't take long. Fully dressed, with white shirt, tweed jacket and brown pants, Riley was cuffed and escorted by Chief Sonne to the police car that waited three stories down in front of the apartment building. Police officers were bringing their equipment into the building, heading up the stairs to his apartment.

They're wasting their time.

An hour later, Chief Sonne was sitting at a table across from Riley, in a closed room at the police station, an officer posted outside the door. He paused for a few moments, sternly looking at his suspect.

Riley, perspiring, put his hand inside his jacket and produced a white handkerchief. Riley saw the Chief flex his muscles in anticipation of an attack, and then relax when he saw the handkerchief. He chuckled under his breath as he dabbed his forehead with the kerchief.

He's afraid of me. Huh, not my type.

The Chief noted his error, but started the conversation as if nothing had happened.

"So, Mr. Nacht, you were at the Roache Boarding School early morning Sunday, January 26, right?"

Riley replaced his kerchief inside his coat pocket. "Yes, that is correct."

"And you were there… why?"

Riley sighed. *Idiot. He knows exactly why.* "It was a star gazing event; perfect time, since there was a moon with a waning crescent at zero visibility to the naked eye, much like a new moon. The stars were nicely aligned over the glass dome of the Roache building. Do you know anything about astronomy, Chief?"

Sonne ignored Riley's evasive maneuver. He used a more aggressive tone. "How long have you lived in Libertyville, Mr. Nacht?"

"About two years."

"Last year on Friday, November 26, 1924 there was a child reported missing. Do you know anything about that, Mr. Nacht?"

"Now, why would I know anything?"

"Was there a new moon that night?"

"I don't remember exactly. There probably was…" Riley yawned.

"The missing child was a girl, about seven years old. Her body was discovered a few weeks later." A pause. Sonne watched Riley carefully. "We never found her head."

Riley yawned again and looked away. "Pity."

"But, we did find a torn handkerchief where her body was tossed, like the one you just used."

Riley smiled. "Lots of people use handkerchiefs."

"Yes, but not all handkerchiefs are used by murderers. Murderers who prefer children; girls in particular, on moonless nights. And, you, Mr. Nacht, are uniquely situated to this opportunity."

Riley shrugged. "You've got nothing on me."

The Chief went on. "Previously, on Tuesday, October 28, 1924. Was there a new moon?"

Riley's reply was sarcastic. "Most probably, yes. It's cyclical, you know."

Chief Sonne ignored the insulting tone. "So, there was a new moon and another missing child. We never found her."

"Too bad."

"But, we found her dress."

"No, you didn't."

Chief Sonne leaned toward Riley, putting his hands on the edge of the table as if looking into his mind. His voice became low in pitch.

"It's something about the cold, the night, no moon and little girls. What does that all mean, Mr. Nacht? How do you know we didn't find her dress?"

Riley laughed. "Because, I just know. You're bluffing."

A knock on the door. "Excuse me." The Chief left the room.

A few moments later, Sonne returned. He was careful to make his way behind Riley while a police officer stood at the doorway watching. "Stand up and place your hands behind your back."

Riley did as he was told and Chief Sonne cuffed him.

"Mr. Nacht, you are being arrested for the murder of Dorothy MacGuire and Lilly-Belle Blake."

"Who?"

"Lilly-Belle Blake. The girl with the missing dress? We found it in the basement of your apartment building; inside the wall, behind the furnace. A brick was loose. Her parents verified that it was their daughter's dress. And we found something else, Mr. Nacht. A pink ribbon wrapped around a lock of strawberry blond hair. Probably Dorothy's hair."

The Chief palmed the lock of strawberry blond hair wrapped in pink ribbon so that Riley could see.

"I want a lawyer."

"Of course, you do."

Four days passed before the rest of Dorothy's body was found. Sitting at his desk at the police station, Chief Sonne reviewed his investigative notes.

The upper torso, sans head, found in a trashed ravine behind a row of Libertyville stores. Lower torso severed at the waist found tucked underneath a gazebo at Butler Lake. The coroner found semen.

The hair on the Chief's neck stood on end as he thought about the coroner's report.

How sick can you get? A twelve-your-old girl...no, a girl's corpse, incomplete. Why violate a corpse?

CHAPTER SEVENTEEN
Secret
1925

Midnight. Warren heard a soft knock on his bedroom door. He rolled over in bed, hoping for more sleep. The knock became louder followed by a sound. "Father?"

His bedroom, thick brocade drapes, thick down comforter, huge bed, handwoven carpet – everything reflected opulence. The mahogany canopy over the bed was held by four large posts. A throne. To the right, windows and access to a balcony. To the left, access to dressing room, closets and bathroom.

Warren moved to the side of his bed and grabbed a robe draped over a nearby chair. "Just a minute." He donned his slippers placed under the chair and turned toward the door. "Come in."

Kimberly opened the door and ran to her father, hugging him.

"What is it?"

"I can't sleep."

He took Kimberly's hand and sat down on the foot of the bed. When she sat next to him he put his arm around her.

"What's on your mind?"

She turned her face into his chest.

He could feel her shiver. "Sometimes when I am afraid, I take a deep breath and just blurt it out."

She raised her face up at him. "You're never afraid."

"Sure, I am. Not so much now, but in my life, I have felt fear."

Kimberly considered this, took a deep breath. "I saw him push Dorothy over the balcony rail."

Warren's eyes went wide, his eyebrows raised, "Is that so? Tell me about it."

"It was the star gazing night. I went with Miss Oberson to put Rose to bed. When I returned to the balcony, I hid behind the curtain. They were whispering. I saw him lift her up and toss her over the railing." Kimberly shivered again.

"Then what happened?"

"I stayed hidden until I heard him leave."

Oh my God! Poor child. "Why did you hide?" Warren asked.

"I don't know why. Something bad. I felt it."

He recalled the nanny's words a few years before. *Sometimes children sense things we adults don't see.*

"Tell me, Kimberly, why didn't you tell this to Miss Oberson?"

"Because I don't like her. She's the one that let the man into the school. It's her fault."

In a way, she's right. From a child's point of view. Gently, Warren asked. "Are you afraid the man will come back?"

Kimberly nodded her head.

"Well, don't be. The man is in jail for life. He can't come here."

"Really?"

Warren's tone reflected finality. "Really. He's gone."

Kimberly pulled away from him. "Can I sleep with you?"

"No, but I'll stay with you in your room until you fall asleep."

He took her hand as they walked to Kimberly's room. He tucked her in, then went around to the other side, sat, and then leaned back against the ornate head board, putting his arm around her pillow.

"There, is that good?"

She cuddled into him. "Un-huh."

"You have nothing to worry about, Kimberly. What's done is done. It really isn't Miss Oberson's fault. It was an unfortunate thing that had happened. Let's not upset the apple cart and talk about it again. Okay?"

Kimberly nodded.

He dosed off for a while, then woke and looked down at her, finally in a deep sleep. *Golly, she's so beautiful. A princess? No. More like a Greek Goddess. There's a power in her.* Warren softly tip-toed out her room and headed for his own bed.

The incident was never discussed again.

CHAPTER EIGHTEEN
What Do We Do?
1925

"What do we do with Mr. Riley Nacht?" Judge Weston of Chicago City gazed at the five men sitting before him in a circle.

To his left was the Defense attorney, and to his right the Prosecuting attorney. Dr. Reed sat next to the Prosecutor. Next to the Defense attorney was the Warden from Joliet Prison, and next to the Warden was Chief Sonne.

The Judge, a fat man with folds of skin hanging from his neck and rosy cheeks, had his nose pointed downward so he could look over his spectacles, eyes moving from face to face. His eyebrows raised, his mouth gaped open, the bulk of his stomach spilling over the top of his pants, belt straining and legs spread apart.

Two weeks prior to this meeting, an initial level of bargaining took place between the defense and prosecuting attorneys. Riley Nacht, at his lawyers bidding, agreed to cooperate with the authorities. During his confession of his murders, the authorities learned of the whereabouts of seven-year-old Wilma's head and how Lilly-Belle Blake was murdered in October and discarded in the Des Plains River.

Riley enjoyed providing the sexual and morbid details of his crimes as if he were reliving moments of pleasure. Chief Sonne was shocked by that and by Riley's apathy towards his victims.

The final judgement was the subject of this meeting. A "guilty" verdict would translate to a life sentence for Mr. Nacht at Joliet Prison. A verdict of "not guilty by reason of insanity" would result with Mr. Nacht being remanded to Elgin State Mental Hospital.

"Well?" Silence. The judge sighed with frustration. "Dr. Reed, what is your assessment of Mr. Riley Nacht?"

"Of course, I'll start. It is my evaluation that Mr. Riley Nacht operates on a very low psychological level. He cannot function in society, so great is his level of disability. It's very unusual that we find him with high intellectual ability, but lacking in simple humanity. He is too impulsive and unpredictable, which makes him dangerous. It's agreed Mr. Nacht cannot return to society. Wherever he goes, it will be a lifetime commitment." He paused, his gaze roving over the massive judge. "Now, Elgin State Mental Hospital is overflowing with patients, and I'll wager the Warden here has the same population problem at Joliet."

Dr. Reed made eye contact with the Warden, who nodded in agreement.

"Then there is a matter of security. This man must be isolated. He cannot associate with other prisoners at Joliet or other patients at Elgin."

"Thank you for mentioning that, Dr. Reed," said the Warden. "Isolation is used in our facility to handle difficult prisoners, but we use it as temporary measure. As a result, the use of isolation is fluid, so our capacity for isolation is almost always at a maximum. Dr. Reed, do you have facilities for isolation?"

"Yes, but it's partial isolation. We call it 'The Hold'. This is where we place extreme cases away from the general populace."

"May I suggest, Dr. Reed..." the Warden paused for a moment to scratch his eye, "...the prisoner be remanded to Elgin for isolation.

You have an opportunity to study the criminal mind – psychopathic, you say?"

"Yes, he is a psychopath. While the opportunity is there, I don't have the resources to study his psychopathic peculiarities, which are unique."

"And I have the man-power at my prison, but don't have the means for isolation at the moment, and I'm not interested in studying his mind." The Warden smiled. "No offense, Sir."

"None taken," replied Dr. Reed, and returned the smile. Then, capitulating, he continued, "Okay, I agree to take Mr. Riley Nacht as a patient at my hospital. I need to know if Joliet Prison can remain an option in some future, if a need comes up."

"Why?" the Judge asked.

"Because the element of danger is too great. You see, this man is ruthless. He knows what society expects from him, but he doesn't care. He has no empathy, no compassion for others. So, he surprises out of a response to a sudden impulse not detectable by others. He'll kill with no warning. If something comes up and I must move Mr. Nacht somewhere, I need to know I can move him to Joliet."

"I agree to that," the Warden gave Dr. Reed an encouraging smile. "We'll work with you as best we can."

Chief Sonne piped in. "I want to have the full Bertillon description of Mr. Riley Nacht before transport."

"Good idea," said the Warden.

Defense raised his eyebrows with concern. "What's a full Bertillon description?"

"It's a thorough physical description of the…" the Chief paused, looking for the right word, "…prisoner using body measurements. It's not just height, weight, hair and eye color. It's head length and width, ears, feet, fingers; it's detailed."

"Why do you need that level of detail?" asked Defense.

"In case we lose him."

Defense nodded.

"Fine," said the Judge. "Does Defense have any concerns?"

"Yes. I want to put this agreement as an addendum to your verdict, Your Honor. In the event Mr. Nacht must be moved, there will be administrative tasks to support a transfer to Joliet."

"Agreed," replied the Judge. "How about Prosecution?"

"No concerns, Your Honor."

"I find, Mr. Riley Nacht, not guilty by reason of insanity and to be remanded at Eglin State Hospital."

The men stood up and relaxed, acknowledging the meeting over. The Warden took out his Lucky Strike cigarettes and offered one to the men. The room was soon filled with smoke and small talk before they headed out the door.

* * *

Two days later, Dr. Reed considered his new patient, Mr. Riley Nacht, recently admitted to maximum security at Elgin State Mental Hospital. Taking his pipe from the pipe stand atop of his desk, he loaded it with his favorite tobacco. While lighting the contents in the bowl, he wondered about this new addition, who was both a new problem and a new opportunity.

*What is a **real** psychopath? It'd be nice if, collectively, we can find a common thread that could help us predict a predisposition toward psychopathic behavior.*

He swiveled his rolling chair away from his desk to the back wall, where his certificates of accomplishments and honorary degrees were displayed. He gazed at them absentmindedly; different vantage points, while he tossed his thoughts around.

Riley is beyond anything we have seen before. Pedophilia and necrophilia is an unusual combination in psychopathic behavior. But then, what is "usual" with a psychopath? Whatever we do for this man, we'll need his cooperation.

He sighed, remembering the awful circumstances of this particular crime.

It was good the poor child, Dorothy, was dead when he decapitated her. I wonder why he did that and why he placed her head on the boarding school gate? Could it be a trophy? Like a lion's head mounted on the wall of the hunter?

Dr. Reed sighed again, this time to expel the feeling of dark energy; a respite, as he looked around his office. He enjoyed the privacy of this space for moments like this. His mahogany desk, his files and books so precious to his research of the mind. Here, he could think things through.

There was a flask of whisky on one of his bookshelves. Retrieving a pony glass from his desk drawer, he poured a drink and took a gulp.

Eccentricity is one of his characteristics, plus brazen nerve, when you think about it. The fact that he stole children away. And especially, Dorothy, killing her right at the school where he would most likely be caught. He's a risk taker... He became more brazen with each kill. The first kill was hidden entirely. The second kill had the body found but no head. He advertised the last kill. Interesting chain of events in a killer's mind. Driven by excitement, the intensity of the moment.

He took another gulp.

Funny how sloppy he was with the evidence. The dress too easily found in the basement of his apartment. Inconsistent? No, infallible, and he wanted it near him. A souvenir.

He downed the rest of the whisky, wipe the glass clean with his handkerchief, and put the glass away.

When we work with him, we'll need to find instances where he is excitable, nervous, compulsive and cold. We need to better understand his eccentricities, especially the sexual perversion part. How did that come about?

The doctor dug deeper.

Copulating with a dead girl's body. The tone of it. He HAD her. He conquered her. Why did he have this drive?

He kicked the notion around more.

I don't have the resources for this. Maybe... just maybe... a preliminary investigation could be done by Eddie Fisk. He's strong and can protect himself. I can direct him how to handle Riley Nacht. I think I'll ask him to do this special service that requires astute handling.

CHAPTER NINETEEN
Eddie
1919

Caleb Fisk, English heritage, was born in 1855 in Virginia. A trader at first, Caleb traveled west and met his wife, a woman from the Chippewa tribe, in Illinois. Their wedding was according to Chippewa custom. They became farmers.

He had four sons with his Chippewa wife. The second child, Samuel, was born in 1882, and he married an English woman, Cornelia. Samuel worked as a laborer for the Illinois Steel Company, making railroad rails, fastenings, and ties.

Samuel and Cornelia begat Edward Lewis Fisk on December 3, 1902. They called him Eddie. He was their only child.

No one knows why Eddie had a deformity in his spine, but it didn't deter him too much. His left shoulder was higher than his right shoulder and left-hand fingers longer than fingers on the right. His jaw was particularly prominent; a trait of Caleb Fisk.

"We are blessed," Cornelia said when she first saw her baby. "He has ten fingers, ten toes, and he has a strong jaw. This boy is a natural leader. Look, Samuel! He has your eyes."

This pleased Samuel.

The child thrived in this tiny family. Samuel, a physically strong man from hard labor, encouraged Eddie to be physically adept as well. Over time, children made fun of Eddie's deformities, but he was always stronger and used his strength to end the torment. His parents never interfered in what they called 'shenanigans', proud that Eddie could hold his own.

It's part of growing up.

Male dominance, where things are settled with a fist.

* * *

One Sunday afternoon, (1915) Samuel took his twelve-year-old son out to a farm owned by Robert Hollar, a man he knew through a fellow at the steel mill. The Hollar's were leasing a prize-winning Hereford bull for mating season.

Mighty nice stock, the bull short and wide, like a brown and white tank with a nice set of horns.

The animal's owner transported the bull in an open stock hauler with bars on the sides and a solid end that doubled as a ramp. They needed to unload the bull, then coax him out to pasture. Not hard work for several men. Just a matter of keeping the animal safe.

The bull's owner drove the truck past the barn to the pasture gate, backing in so that when the ramp opened, the animal could walk down the plank and head out toward the cows. Men held fencing along the exposed sides of the pasture opening so the bull couldn't double back and escape.

Inside the pasture a few cows chewed their cud, not showing any alarm.

A man climbed up the truck and opened the ramp.

The bull wouldn't leave the truck.

"Hey, Hollar!" shouted a man, "play some soft music, get him in the mood for romance."

The men laughed.

"Use this to poke him on the rear end, get'em going." A man handed a long stick to Eddie. Eddie looked up at his father.

"C'mon, Son." He grabbed one end, walked up to the hauler and poked the bull's thigh. The bull gave Eddie a glance and stood still.

"Harder!"

Eddie gave him a strong whack on the lower back. The bull moved forward, walked down the ramp and trotted out to the field.

Hollar shouted, "Let's see if the ladies take to him."

The men watched him make his way to the cows. Some ran away; a couple stayed their place. Sniffing, peeing, all the rituals of bovine courtship, and finally it happened. The bull mounted a cow, pumped a few times, and then stayed motionless for a moment before he released her.

Applause and laughter. "Where are the cigarette's?" someone shouted.

The truck pulled away a few feet and someone closed the pasture gate. All was well.

On their way back home, Samuel asked Eddie, "Do you understand what happened out there? God made males and females. When they get together like that bull did, after a time, a baby comes out. It's the birds and the bees, Son. That's how life is made."

"Is that how I was made?"

"Yep. Your mother and I made you. That's what married folks do and God decides what child comes out."

Eddie felt a mixture of curiosity and fascination. He often wondered why women looked the way they did with breasts, small waists and wide hips. His mother's body, so much rounder and soft than his father's, which was more square, bulky with muscle.

Samuel could see the wheels churning in the boy's head from the corner of his eye as he was driving home.

"That's why women bleed once a month. It's part of how babies are made."

Eddie recalled the towels, stained from menstruation, his mother laundered, never fully understanding why they were needed. A few times he gaged when saw them soiled, but he never asked about it.

"Do you have questions?"

A pause. "So how did you and mom meet?"

"I met her at a picnic. We knew the same people. I got to talk to her. We got along and so I met her kin and, over time, I asked her to marry me."

Silence. *I wonder if there will ever be a wife for me.*

That was a sore spot for Eddie. Girls avoided him, not making eye contact. And he didn't understand their female gibberish and silly giggling. He decided they were too stupid, but then, later, couldn't figure out how to approach a girl. In other ways, he reasoned, they were complicated. He finally decided to retreat from them all together.

Life is easier that way.

By the time 1918 rolled around, and Eddie was fifteen years old. The famous Al Capone was making headlines in Chicago for bootlegging, prostitution and gambling. All a hub-bub with energy, the Chicago and Libertyville populace, both aghast and amused by the gangster life style. People couldn't stop talking about it.

Al Capone, Johnny Torrio, "Bugs" Moran made a strong impression on Eddie. The money, the power, and the gangster fights. To Eddie, the mob was glorious. Exciting, living on the edge. And the women, discarded harlots.

There it was again – the problem: females.

Samuel noticed Eddie's struggle with females; his clumsy shyness toward them. He took matters into his own hands.

"Son, I have something for you." They had just finished lunch on a Sunday afternoon. "Let's take a walk."

"Where are you going?" asked Cornelia, as she picked up the dishes from the kitchen table and placed them in the kitchen sink.

"Out."

Eddie looked at his mom. Her bluish right eye, something she acquired during house work, almost healed, and the swelling of her upper lip almost gone. He shrugged his shoulders at her and followed his father.

Cornelia knew not to ask more questions. *Men do things, sometimes, that women need not know.*

She sighed, suspecting that Samuel was going to introduce their young teenage son to an element of manhood. She let out a breath, shaking her head with mixed feelings. *It's a man's world.*

She touched her eye carefully as if to further sooth the pain subsiding. Eddie did not know Samuel had delivered the blow.

They did not chat. Eddie simply followed his father as they took a trolley to another part of town. Their destination: a brothel. Eddie had never seen one before, though he heard about them. It was a wooden two-story structure. Simple. It looked clean, but one could see the building needed repair. Peeling paint and a broken window shutter.

Samuel knocked on the door. Eddie silently observed his father as he talked to the matron.

"He's a virgin. I'm looking for someone who is clean, patient and can teach him."

The matron, gaudy with too much makeup and wearing a lace robe that revealed her ample breasts, smiled at Eddie.

"Come in…" She stepped aside, gesturing for them to enter, and then she closed the door. A stairway leading to the second floor was directly in front of them.

"I have just the girl for you," she smiled at Eddie. "She's your age, too. She'll make sure you have a good time."

Eddie didn't know what to say. He watched as his father negotiate the price with the woman and give her money. Then he looked to the right. They were standing next to an empty living room that had a tapestry on the wall and a couch placed on a throw rug. He noticed a tangy odor, earthy, like human sweat. There was a wet bar at the far wall.

His attention was interrupted when a young girl appeared in the room from a door adjacent to the wet bar. She was black with tight braids woven closely to her scalp. The garment she wore was too big for her. She looked down at her bare feet, too sheepish for eye contact.

"Are you kidding me?" Samuel glared at the matron.

"You get what you pay for."

"We can go somewhere else."

"Now, don't be hasty. I have another girl you might be interested in."

The matron looked at the black girl. "Nelly, get Sofia."

The door swung open, Nelly left and Sofia entered. The males were struck by Sofia's dominate trait: long, thick, and frizzy red hair in disarray, as if it had been wind-blown. She had a spray of freckles that danced across her face and framed her emerald eyes.

Samuel watched her expression, shocked at first, when she made eye contact with Eddie, and then there was a questioning look toward the matron, who nodded back.

Samuel was delighted. Eddie stood frozen and the matron gave her pitch.

"She's seventeen years old, healthy as a horse and doctor certified." She chuckled. "He was just here yesterday. I have my girls checked every week. She knows what to do."

Sofia wore a white silk slip that dipped down to reveal the modest cleavage of her small breasts. The length of the slip fell just above her dainty feet, clad in white sandals. She smoothly dropped the right strap of her garment, further revealing her right breast. Then, she looked at Eddie and struck an inviting pose for him.

Eddie, now wide-eyed, looked at Samuel. It was obvious to his father what his son now wanted.

"How much?"

"Double."

"How much, say, for thirty minutes?"

"Double."

Samuel felt trapped between the price and his desire to introduce his son to women. He struggled with empathy for Eddie's difficulty. His concern was deep, acknowledging Eddie was particularly challenged, viewed too ugly for women to give him a chance. He looked from Eddie to the striking redhead.

She is pretty. First time for him, too.

"Alright."

He handed the matron his money while Sofia walked to Eddie, took his hand and led him up the stairs.

"Thank you," said the matron, taking his money. "Would you like to sit and have a drink while you wait?"

"Sure," Samuel said. He made his way to the couch and sat down.

"Bourbon or whiskey?"

"Whiskey."

"That'll be ten cents." The matron smiled.

An hour later, Eddie skipped down the stairs and found his father waiting for him in the living room. Eddie was beaming, wearing a smile on his face as wide as the sun. Samuel, got up from the couch, put his arms around Eddie's shoulders and led him out the door, happy for his son.

They never spoke of this incident. A closely held secret between men.

CHAPTER TWENTY
The Talk
1926

The students at Roache Boarding School had finally settled into a calm routine, the ghastly past events fading from memory. It was all about the future now. Exciting and hopeful.

The girls chatted quietly as they sat in the classroom waiting for Miss Oberson to arrive. This was a special class for budding young women with the need to learn about notable body changes that nature would shortly provide.

The room was comfortably designed for such delicate matters. The chairs padded and placed around a coffee table. A chalkboard to one side, and an easel for displaying pictures. The room was painted a soft blue with white molding. The carpet flowered, colors muted. Single standing lamps with white lace shades and oil paintings of roses and lilacs provided a soft tone to encourage feminine calm. Victorian.

On an opposite wall of the entrance was a chest of drawers made of inlaid wood. The girls wondered what it contained. A bowl of sachet was set on top. Above it hung a mirror with an ornate frame. A lilac scent filled the room. Calming.

Miss Oberson, wearing a black dress with long sleeves, came into the room and paused to survey her students.

Her light brown hair tied back in a bun, her hair framing her face. She wore a gold chain and earrings, which made her look elegant. Her shoes had a raised heal. She sashayed when she walked. Under her arm she held a large folder with thick paper inside.

"Good morning, ladies."

The five girls responded in unison, "Good morning, Miss Oberson."

She admired her audience. "My, you all look beautiful!" She closed the door.

Indeed. Each child was impeccably dressed in current 1920's twelve-year-old fashion. School regulation insisted. The girls nodded approvingly to each other.

Miss Oberson gazed for a moment at Kimberly's new dress. *Deep purple – a striking color for her!*

Kimberly noticed Miss Oberson's gaze so she tilted her chin posing.

Miss Oberson put the folder down on the coffee table and sat down, her hands in her lap, back straight.

"Today, we'll discuss the miracle of life, gender and procreation. It's natural to be uncomfortable, even embarrassed, but these are things you need to know. It's part of being an adult."

The girls looked at each other with mixed feelings.

"This conversation is also very private. What is discussed here is to be held in confidence. Our conversation is just among us ladies. Agreed?"

In unison, "Yes, Miss Oberson."

"Okay. Now we will begin. Of course, you have noticed the difference between girls and women. When a female develops into a woman, her body changes. The most obvious are breasts and hips. Rather than the straight body line of a child, females become curvy. Other changes occur, too. Body hair, for instance, under the arms, on legs and in your private area between your legs."

She reached inside the folder and produced a paper that was passed around. It was a sketch of an anatomically correct naked woman.

"When your breasts start to develop you may experience discomfort."

A raised hand.

"You don't need to raise your hand while we discuss this. I want our conversation to be relaxed."

"Is *that* what's happening? I'm sore here." Jane indicated her chest.

"Yes. So, I brought some pictures of brassieres. Here's one you might like, Jane. Please pass this around." The paper displayed pictures of different support undergarments. Miss Oberson pointed to a suitable lace bra for Jane.

"Why do we wear these?"

"To hold our breasts up."

"Why do we want to hold our breasts up?"

"So, they don't flop around. They stay in place. It's more comfortable."

Miss Oberson was pleased with the mood of her girls. They were curious, non-judgmental and relaxed. *Perfect.*

"Regarding our privates," she pointed to the picture, "the difference between females and males is anatomy. Females have a private space, a hallowed place. It's called 'vagina'. Males have a protuberant appendage. It's called 'penis'."

She passed around a sketch of an anatomically correct nude man. The girls raised their eyebrows, wondering, too uncomfortable to say anything. The picture was passed around quickly. The last girl placed it on the coffee table face down.

"Now, here is another picture showing what is *inside* a female body. You can see the uterine tubes, uterus and vagina. Notice how the end of a uterine tube looks like branches of a tree. This is where female eggs are. Once a month, an egg is released and travels through the uterine tube, into the uterus and out the vagina. When this happens, you will see blood."

A gasp! *What?*

Miss Oberson waited as the girls digested this information. In her experience, this was the first of two difficult parts of her lecture. She slowed down the pace.

A question. "Blood? Will I die?"

"No. This naturally happens to all women."

Miss Oberson checked the girl's reaction to see if they were ready to move on. *Yes, they're ready.*

"We certainly can't be hindered with this God-given inconvenience, so there is a solution. It's a sanitary absorbent pad made by Kotex. I have a special box for each of you."

Miss Oberson walked to the dresser, retrieved five boxes and passed them around. Each box, made of heavy cardboard, was decorated in a pink carnation flower motif. A ribbon was attached to the top and bottom and tied into a bow. Delicate.

"Go ahead, open them up."

The girls untied the bows and opened the boxes. Inside were smaller boxes of individual Kotex pads. There were also two small envelopes each containing a belt. There was a pink safety pin and an instruction pamphlet. The presentation was very sweet.

"Let's review the pamphlet."

Obediently, each child read out loud a paragraph from the pamphlet. When they finished Miss Oberson asked, "Are there any questions?"

None. "Good. Now there's more to discuss."

More?

She challenged them. "Why do you think God made this happen?" No answer. "Briefly, the sperm from a male fertilizes the female's egg. That's how babies are made."

A moment passed. "A baby grows inside the woman's uterus. Nine months later, a baby is born. Have you seen a pregnant woman?"

Some nodded yes.

"Sometimes women prefer to stay at home during this time. Discretion is always a correct choice."

Little Susan, the smallest of the girls, asked, "So, how does the sperm get to the egg?"

Ah, the second difficult part of this session.

"When a man and a woman get married, they become one physically. The male's penis enters the woman's vagina. He deposit's his sperm into her body. This is called 'intercourse'."

The girls were shocked. Miss Oberson stifled her own reaction to the tell-tale expressions on these innocent young faces. Horror!

"Hell, no!" said little Susan.

Miss Oberson looked at Susan sternly. "Ladies of culture do not use profanity!" Then, she softened. "Really. There's no reason to be alarmed. For heavens sakes. This has to do with love."

"My father doesn't love my mother and I have two sisters!"

Miss Oberson, again, refrained from laughing by taking her kerchief and dabbing her nose.

"Well…assuming marriage happens when a man and a woman fall in love, the coupling is a wonderful experience."

"How do you know? You're not married."

Susan is honest as the day is long, but is so persistent!

Miss Oberson subtilty projected an air of Victorian propriety – sitting up a tad straighter, her nose raised. "I've been told this." Then, adjusted her tone. "Have you ever felt close to someone? A sister, a friend, a family member?"

Some of the girls nodded.

"Someday, when you fall in love with a man, you'll feel good inside. You'll want to be with him. You might hold hands at first, gaze into each other's eyes. You might let him kiss you on the cheek. Later, your lips may touch in a brief kiss. It happens naturally. Courtship. But ladies, always hold off on any other physical advances until married. You save yourself for your husband."

A pause while the children considered the idea of love.

"Why aren't you married?"

"I was in love once, but his family insisted he marry another woman."

Susan said, "That's what happened to my father."

Miss Oberson smiled. "Sometimes marriages have to do with duty, obligation. The best marriages, I think, are when a man and a woman love each other. Know the children from all marriages are always cherished by their parents. You are God's gift."

Another child contributed to the discussion. "I think I understand now when my mother tells my father her period is here."

Miss Oberson laughed. "Yes. 'Period' is a good name for it."

A third child asked, "Does it hurt?"

Perplexed, Miss Oberson asked, "Does what hurt? Developing breasts? Menstruation? Giving birth?"

"Coupling. When a man and a woman get together."

"I've been told it is wonderful, loving, intimate. Two hearts beating as one. The best poetry is written about this kind of love. *Romeo and Juliet*, for example."

The girls felt reassured, more accepting of their talk. Miss Oberson looked at her Elgin wrist watch. "We've been here for two hours. Is there any other discussion? Any questions?"

"May I tell my mother we had this talk?"

"Yes, of course. It's good for you to talk to your mother about this. Anything else?"

No response. "Just one last thing. We never have a discussion like this in mixed company. This is a private female subject, so we keep it among ourselves, among women."

The girls in unison, "Thank you, Miss Oberson."

"You're quite welcome," she replied and smiled.

Kimberly followed the other girls out of the room with mixed feelings.

I don't have any one to talk to.

* * *

Warren received a handwritten note from Roache Boarding School.

Dear Mr. Warren Weatherspoon,

> *This letter is to inform you of a very discreet meeting I have had with a small collection of Roache girls entering puberty. Miss Kimberly Luc Weatherspoon was a participant in this discussion.*

> *The purpose of this meeting was to prepare these young novices of adulthood for upcoming physical changes they*

will soon experience. We also talked about the mysteries of life and social propriety.

I feel a deep responsibility to inform you of this since it influences the successful future of your daughter, Kimberly. This discussion has occurred and Kimberly received the information well.

Please let me know if you have any questions or concerns.

Very Truly Yours,

Miss Oberson, Head Mistress of Roache Boarding School

Warren was impressed. A stickler subject had been astutely handled by a lady with whom he had entrusted the care of his daughter.

By golly, sending her to Roache was a good thing!

He looked at the letter again, admiring the fine paper, the exquisite hand writing. A piece of art.

Very nice. Truly, very nice.

Warren had decided the time was right for him to have a private chat with his daughter. They were in his office at the Weatherspoon mansion. Kimberly sat in a chair in front of his desk.

He fumbled. *How to begin.*

"Kimberly, I received information from Miss Oberson that you have had a talk about the mysteries of life."

Kimberly was surprised she told her father. "She said this was a conversation between ladies."

"Quite so. I'm very pleased that she had that discussion with you and some other young ladies."

He cleared his throat. "I suppose she explained that men and women in society are different."

Kimberly nodded.

"Well, men in our station of life sometimes require female attention in privacy."

Kimberly furrowed her eyes. *What does he mean?*

He noted her expression. "You see, healthy men need women in their lives. Women, on the other hand, should be chaste for their husbands. This is a message that Roache teaches, but I also want to reinforce this idea to you. This is also what society requires, particularly of women in this station of life. High society is not always easy. There are expectations."

"Was my mother chaste?"

"Oh, yes. I would not have married her had she not been. You see, men of wealth and power require the best. The best women are chaste."

He retrieved a pony glass from a drawer and poured a drink. "So, there is a rule I want to explain. You are not to come to my bedroom – ever. That's off limits."

"Why, Father? You come to my bedroom."

"That's okay for me. It's not okay for you."

"Why?"

"Because I'm the man of this house and I may not be alone. I may not want to be disturbed."

"Will I know who is with you?"

"No."

"I don't understand."

"You will in time."

"But what if I need you, Father? Why can't I knock on your bedroom door?"

"If you need me for something, ask William. Either he will handle it or he'll get me for you. So, with this arrangement, I am letting your nanny go."

"You mean no more nannies?" *What a relief!*

"That's right. You're older now. I think Roache is doing well for you. You are becoming quite grown up. When you are home, we have this rule. I don't see a need for a nanny."

He looked at his daughter with warmth, pushed back his chair and reached his arms out to her. She ran to him for an embrace.

CHAPTER TWENTY-ONE
Job Application
1926

With his schooling completed, Eddie found a job at the Illinois Steel Company, but hated the work being stuck in a position of high risk-taking, long hours and minimal pay. He had heard Elgin State Mental Hospital was in need of men with strong backs, because the patient population had grown with the end of The Great War (WWI). He applied for a job as a hospital assistant and was interviewed by Dr. Reed.

The multi-purpose room where they sat was located on the ground floor of the doctor's offices building. Dr. Reed chose to use this room for the convenience of hospital applicants, knowing it would be easy to find.

Eddie had no idea how auspicious his interviewer was, but he sensed it, facing Dr. Reed as he sat across from him at the long table.

Dr. Nigel Reed was considered an outstanding leader in his field. He had served his community as President of the Chicago Neurological Society and President of the Illinois Psychiatric Society. He created new ways to treat the mentally infirm, and eventually became a leader of chemical shock therapy. To the people who knew him well, Dr. Reed understood the dynamics, the conundrum, in the human mind.

The doctor considered Eddie's appearance.

Nice suit, well shaven, hesitant man. Looks me in the eye. Good. Physical deformities. Has confidence. Probably strong. Might be a good candidate. Looks to be in his early twenties.

Eddie observed Dr. Reed.

Medium build, balding hair, spectacles, thin. Probably spends too much time with books. Sits in chairs a lot. Not physically adept. Intelligent.

"Let me introduce myself. I am Dr. Reed, a psychiatrist and Superintendent of this hospital. You must be Mr. Eddie Fisk."

"Yes. How do you do?"

"I'm fine, thank you. I appreciate your application for Hospital Assistant. Please tell me, why did you apply for this job?"

Get to the point.

"Sure. I work at the Illinois Steel Company as a laborer. While I do the job well, I'd like to work here, Sir, to get a different experience in life. Factory labor work is boring, routine, with no future. I want a future. I want to use my back less and my brain more."

Dr. Reed smiled. *I like his honesty.*

"So, why didn't you go to college?"

"My folks can't afford to send me to college."

"Did you take an I.Q. test?"

"Yes."

"Score?"

"130."

Good score. I'll check that.

"Did you school here locally?"

"Yes."

"Can you give me a name?"

"Mrs. Sandra Prusik."

"What subjects did you study?"

"Typical subjects: geography, history, algebra, physiology, rhetoric, and philosophy."

"Fine. So, what are your aspirations?"

"I'm interested in psychology. If I work here, I expect to find opportunities where I can learn; maybe go to college part-time."

"Good idea. I like that. The job is very physically demanding. Is that a problem for you?"

Eddie smirked. "It can't be as hard as working a steel mill."

Dr. Reed smiled. "I expect so. The physical demands are probably not as constant. However, we handle people who sometimes don't think clearly. They squirm, become difficult and sometimes fight back. Do you think you can handle that?"

"Yes."

Hmmm. Temperament. "So, give me an example where you handled a difficult person or a challenging event?"

"It happened during a baseball game. I was the team captain and the short stop got hurt from a fly ball. He got mad, went after the pitcher, but I calmed him down. We went on with the game."

"Thank you, Mr. Fisk. What I'd like to do now is tell you about our hospital and our patients. We serve a large community of people who come from Elgin, Libertyville and surrounding areas. Our facility is large, with over twelve hundred beds. Our patients include men, women and children. Some are war veterans, others are folks with varying medical, psychiatric and psychological aliments. We do as best we can to help them become normal, functioning people and return them back to society. But there are those who are life-long inhabitants. We try to make use of patient living here and ask them to work and help keep this facility running, while we give them care."

"That's a big job," Eddie said.

"Yes, it is. I'm glad you see it that way. So, the job is multi-faceted. It includes being open to learning new things, new concepts and procedures. Communication is key. Frankly, a mild temperament is required. We'll ask you to take classes and make use of our mentors. The job requires you do the lowest task, such as cleaning up after a patient, which might be revolting in nature, as well as more challenging tasks. We expect that whatever is asked, is executed exceptionally well. We foster a strong sense of responsibility and accountability here. This is what makes our facility notable."

Eddie, engaged with Dr. Reed's words, started to realize the extent of this job.

"Now I know why the job title is Hospital Assistant. The tasks are many and varied."

Dr. Reed nodded. "That's right. Now, I'll tell you what we tell new doctors coming into our hospital. This will give you an idea of how we treat our patients.

We first examine the patient physically and psychologically per hospital pre-admittance standards to determine or confirm diagnosis and prognosis. Generally, if the symptomatic behavior of the patient is mild, we first try a non-invasive approach for cure. The patient may get information and perspective to make his own behavioral adjustment. If agreement is achieved, and his behavior has changed for the better, we can claim the patient cured.

If that approach doesn't work, then we pursue simple prescriptions such as cold baths and restraint, using a strait jacket, since these are easy to implement and are short-lived. We look to see if this strategy opens a door of opportunity for the patient to make their own changes, by providing information and a perspective that leads to health.

If these approaches do not work toward change for the better, then invasive approaches are recommended. Narcotics can be used sparingly, or insulin shock therapy.

Lastly, the most expensive, but also the most likely to achieve positive results, is lobotomy. Candidates for this approach are carefully screened and must be approved by our team of doctors.

If we cannot cure, then imprisonment might be required, such that we protect society first. In these cases, we can conduct some studies that may help us pre-determine abnormal behavior or criminal behavior. The goal is to predict aberrations and deviants circumventing unwelcome events and intervention.

Lastly, there are the folks who will never be cured, but need our hospital services. The elderly, those who are not ambulatory, and those who are destitute, usually with incurable conditions such as dementia or syphilis.

For those we can help, each prescribed approach is reviewed by our team of staff doctors. We want to verify results to determine effectiveness and gather statistics.

Do you have questions?"

"Yes. For those criminals, are the police involved?"

"Sometimes. Of course, we need to know about the patient – what they did and what brought them here. Criminologists come here to study their discipline. Investigators may want to interview someone living here. We have a good relationship with the local authorities. Why do you ask?"

"I might be interested in that. Frankly, Dr. Reed, I see a lot of opportunities here."

"I do, too. Well, Mr. Fisk, I must conclude our interview. Are there any other questions?"

"Yes. When will I hear from you?"

"By the end of the week. Anything else?"

"No."

Dr. Reed extended his hand as he stood up from his chair. "Thank you very much for coming."

"Thank you, Sir. I look forward to working here."

A few days later, Eddie received a job offer from Dr. Reed at Elgin State Mental Hospital. It appeared to Samuel and Cornelia Fisk their son had found his niche in life. He was healthy, he had a job with a future at the hospital, and he was self-sufficient.

The only thing he didn't yet have was a woman of his own.

CHAPTER TWENTY-TWO
Eddie Meets Riley
1926

Eddie closed Dr. Reeds door and walked down the hall with his hands in his pant pockets, head down, as he considered the doctor's words regarding Mr. Riley Nacht. He compensated for the tilt of his left shoulder by hunching over forward. This made him look like the Hunchback of Notre-Dame – the cruel tease from childhood, but it was comfortable for him to move that way. Occasionally, he scratched the whiskers on his prominent chin, the stubble sandpaper thick. His heavy eyebrows furrowed.

He descended three flights of stairs in the physician's office building at Elgin State Mental Hospital, glad Dr. Reed entrusted him with sensitive information regarding this particular patient. An honest-to-God psychopathic murderer, something of a wonder. Intriguing, but alarming. The man too intelligent. So, the problem was three-fold; a mentally insane patient, physically strong, and cunning.

Eddie reached the ground floor, walked past the receptionist's desks and exited the building. He buttoned up his jacket against the cold March afternoon. The trees, still bare from winter, stood among scattered hyacinths, forsythia and daffodils, the hope of spring, on the Elgin State Mental Hospital grounds. The air refreshingly brisk.

He considered his interview, fifteen minutes ago, with Dr. Reed.

"I'm glad you are willing to do this service for me, Eddie. You'll be an extension of my care for this patient. I hope you like that idea."

Eddie had been sitting in a wooden chair opposite of Dr. Reed, the doctor's large mahogany desk between them. He tried not to stare at the framed degrees and credentials hanging on the wall behind the doctor's rolling chair of padded leather.

"I'm glad to help out any way I can."

"I appreciate that. But, Eddie, you must be alert when you are with this patient. He is impulsive. If you strike a nerve with him, he may attack you. Sometimes psychopaths are amazingly strong. The neurotransmitters in the brain release a chemical, so be careful."

"Yes, Sir, I will."

"Fine. So, spend time when you can fit it in your day. About thirty minutes. Ask about his parents, his back ground. We already have his professional and educational history, so we don't need that. We're looking for his familial history and personal experiences, friends he may have had – pets, things like that. Report to me when you have something. As things progress, we'll adjust the time you spend with him, or I might take over. If you can do this initial ground work that will help out with our patient load."

"I'm happy to do this, Sir."

The doctor extended his right hand to him.

"Thank you, Eddie. I appreciate it. Your extra service will be noted on your record."

Eddie glanced at his Elgin wrist watch as he walked. *Three-fifteen. Okay, I'll see this Mr. Riley Nacht now.*

He picked up his pace and walked four more blocks through the Elgin State Mental Hospital grounds to the maximum-security building for men called '*The Hold*'. It had the appearance of a prison, having bars on the windows and a guard at the entrance. The concrete oblong building, foreboding, three stories high.

Eddie flashed his badge at an Elgin Hospital Security Guard as protocol demanded. The guard, dressed in a dark blue uniform, nodded and let him enter. Eddie noticed the barred windows on either side of the double front door as he entered. Sunshine glowed through the windows and onto the gray tiled floor, leaving distorted shadows of window panes and bars.

The stark gray lobby walls surrounded a single desk in the center of the lobby, manned by another guard. Eddie imagined the guard's face as gray also, even though he wore a dark blue uniform. There were gray metal chairs next a wall on the left. Straight ahead the staircase. The guard office to the right, with inside glass windows protected by iron bars. The door to this room locked. If one looked carefully through the window, one could see a rack of stored rifles, hand guns, hand cuffs, strait jackets and police sticks at the far end of the guard room.

Eddie gave the guard his badge, which the Elgin Hospital Security Guard took and looked at, as he made an entry in his log bound in gray leather.

"I'm here to see Mr. Riley Nacht."

"In the basement." The guard motioned with a shrug of his shoulder at the staircase behind him. "Last cell on the left. Before you go, please sign here."

He handed his log to Eddie, indicating his required signature. The guard saw Eddie's left hand was different than his right, eyebrows raised in surprise. He handed Eddie's badge back to him when Eddie had finished signing the log. Eddie sighed over the guard's reaction, used to folks who sometimes looked at him funny.

"Thank you."

He made his way down two flights of stairs, passed through a heavy door and entered a large hall with cells on both sides. *Last one on the left.*

This was a small unit for extreme cases, when security preempted other concerns. The men, scraggly and thin, watched him walk down the aisle. Eddie ignored them, but found it hard to ignore the stench.

"Hey, Buddy, got a smoke?"

Taunting whistles. "Hey, Honey, c'mon over here and talk to me."

Eddie walked on. From the corner of his eye, he caught a patient wearing a straightjacket laying on the floor of his cell. He hastened his pace.

Riley heard the commotion, stood up from his cot and leaned against the bars on the front of his cell.

Eddie arrived at his destination, and took in this patient, this Riley person. Tall and thin, with a receding hairline and thin white hair at the sides and violet eyes. An albino. He wore blue denim pants and a white undershirt. His feet were bare.

The tidy cell had a wash bin and a toilet. There were three books stacked on a table top. The prisoner's closet had no doors. Shirts and pants hung on hooks, underwear and socks folded underneath. The cell window with bars was high up, since the cell was mostly underground. Intentionally architected for security.

"Are you Riley Nacht?"

"Yes. Who are you?"

"I'm Eddie Fisk. I work for Dr. Reed. Can we have a talk?"

"Well, I'm not *going* anywhere."

"Okay then. Dr. Reed asked me to spend time with you. Chat a bit."

"Ah, so you're his stand-in, his go-between."

"Yes. Is that okay with you?"

"What's in it for me?"

"A break in monotony."

Riley sniggered and relaxed. "So, what do you want to know?"

"Just some basic things. Tell me where you come from."

"What does that matter?"

Eddie paused, not responding.

"I'm from New York. My parents came to this country from Germany before The Great War broke out."

Eddie heard the edge in Riley's voice. "Do you have brothers, sisters?"

"Nope."

"How did you become an astronomer?"

"I did well academically. I didn't go to the stars. The stars came to me."

"Do the stars speak to you?"

Riley laughed. "No." *Cynicism.* "Do they speak to you?"

"What I meant was, what is it about the night sky that grabbed your attention?"

"Well, there's a lot of things in the universe – up there." Riley crossed his arms and motioned with his head toward the sky. "Things you wouldn't understand. Celestial mysteries, science, mythology and the gods."

Riley waited to see Eddie's reaction. Under normal circumstances, he wouldn't care, but now, in a maximum-security dormitory, he was interested.

"The god's, huh?"

"Yeah, huh," Riley mimicked, then changed his tone. "There is a pattern of fate reflected in the stars; the *'fall of the dice'*, *'the turn of the wheel'*, some would say. The power of the gods is not observed by most people, because they're too wrapped up in their own pitiful, short-sighted minds. They cannot see omnipotence at work."

"But you can."

"Yep."

"And your work made you appreciate that even more."

Riley did not expect that. Non-judgmental and accurate.

Eddie felt this was a good place to end the conversation, since he had other things to do.

"Okay…well…good chatting with you. I'll be back tomorrow."

"Sure, you will, kid. Don't worry if I'm not here. I have a golfing date."

Eddie let Riley's attitude slide. *Figure he's about ten years older than me…*

He turned away, walked down the aisle toward the prison door, and disappeared from Riley's sight.

His itinerary that day included laundry, which meant working with his male patients in their dormitory, making sure they washed their own clothes and linens. He slapped one seventeen-year-old across the face when the young man refused to do "women's work".

"You're here and you'll do what I tell you!" Eddie's eyes bored into the young man's face. Hate mixed with resentment, but the teenager complied.

The afternoon included monitoring craft work by patients that had woodworking skills. The idea was to keep able-bodied members of the community working. This alleviated hospital labor pressures while keeping patients busy in their own program for mental health.

Later, Eddie told Dr. Reed about his conversation with Riley Nacht.

"You did fine," the doctor reassured him. "Looks like you touched on something that resonates with him. Keep at it."

At the time, Dr. Reed was not aware how accurate his words would become.

CHAPTER TWENTY-THREE
How The Gods Played
1926

The Doctor's Office Building was two miles north-west of the original main building at Elgin State Mental Hospital. The four-story building accommodated the needs of the physicians, patients and visiting families. Individual doctor offices included a private waiting room, with each office decorated to individual taste. Each floor had lavatories and a private meeting room. The entryway contained two desks and two receptionists sharing a phone and schedule. Functional, comfortable, it worked well for the staff administering to the patient population.

The oblong meeting room was bright with morning sunlight. Shadowed window panes were outlined on a mahogany table top. Dr. Hoshkins, sitting at the head, had a cup of coffee in front of him. Doctors Thiele and Manning were sitting on either side of Hoshkins.

It was a typical morning meeting for Dr. Reed and his staff.

A gentleman in his forties, wearing a dark gray suit, opened the meeting room door. He wore his wire-framed glasses on the end of his nose, lowering his chin to look over the rims. He had a long narrow face, flushed red and bloated, a testament to his alcoholic activities. His ruddy complexion and curly red hair suggested an Irish heritage.

"Hello, I am Dr. Brenner. Dr. Reed told me to attend this meeting."

Dr. Hoshkins guessed his age to be about thirty.

This must be the gentleman Dr. Reed spoke of...a new hire.

Dr. Brenner entered and started to close the door when Dr. Reed suddenly appeared and grabbed the door to enter the room. The two men laughed, having avoided a collision.

Dr. Reed started the meeting as he closed the door.

"Good morning, gentlemen. Let me introduce you to Dr. Brenner. He is a psychiatrist from the Cherokee State Hospital and has become a new member of our staff. Dr. Brenner, let me introduce you to Doctors Thiele, Manning and Hoshkins."

Looking at the newcomer, he added, "Dr. Brenner, why don't you sit next to me."

He moved to the long side of the table where there were two empty wooden chairs with leather backing and seats, facing Doctors Thiele and Manning. Dr. Brenner followed him and the two men adjusted their chairs and sat down.

"Let's introduce ourselves. Dr. Hoshkins, why don't you start."

"Of course," said Dr. Hoshkins. "I completed my medical residency at Johns Hopkins School of Medicine. I was an assistant to Dr. Walter Dandy during many of his neurosurgeries. Now, I'm a psychiatrist and a neurosurgeon."

Dr. Brenner appreciated that association with the famous Dr. Walter Dandy spoke to outstanding personal accomplishment. He also knew there were few neurosurgeons in the medical profession.

"That's impressive," Dr. Brenner said to Dr. Hoshkins, who sipped his coffee.

"I'm Dr. Thielie. I did my residency at the New York State Psychiatric Institute. I've been practicing psychiatry for fifteen years. The last five years have been here."

"Glad to meet you," Dr. Brenner nodded, making eye contact with Dr. Thiele.

"I'm Dr. Manning. I've been practicing psychiatry for ten years. My residency was at St. Elizabeth's Hospital in Washington D.C."

"That's a huge hospital. I'm sure you had some very interesting cases, Doctor."

"Well, yes. Our facility here is just as large. You will see, Dr. Brenner, we have quite a variety of patients with various illnesses."

"I'm sure."

Dr. Reed turned away from the table and sneezed. He reached into the pocket of his tweed suit coat to retrieve a handkerchief.

"Excuse me. Why don't you tell us more about yourself, Dr. Brenner?" He wiped his nose with the white cloth.

"I'm from Iowa, Carver College of Medicine. My residency was at Independence State Hospital. I've been practicing psychiatry for eight years. My wife and I have just moved here. We have a little girl, age ten. That's about it."

Dr. Reed sneezed again, this time into the soft white fabric.

"Okay. So, Dr. Brenner, we meet here every morning, Monday through Thursday, to discuss some of our patients or any concerns we may have. The meeting can last for an hour or fifteen minutes, depending upon demands. Sometimes, when there is too much going on, our morning meeting may be cancelled. You can check with my secretary to verify cancellation."

Another sneeze.

"Excuse me. I think it's allergies." A pause. "Of course, everything said in this room is strictly confidential. Some cases require we work as a team. I make that decision. In most cases, your patients are your responsibility."

"I appreciate that," Dr. Brenner replied.

Dr. Reed pocketed his handkerchief.

"I'd like you to spend the next few days with Dr. Manning. We'll determine what patients will be assigned to you at the end of the week.

"That's fine."

"Now, for today's agenda. I have taken on a new patient, a criminal psychopath, Mr. Riley Nacht. He's thirty-three years old and lives alone. He is an astronomer from the University of Chicago and has worked at the Elgin National Watch Company observatory. He can be delightful when conversing about the stars and planets. That's his bailiwick. He is a pedophile with some sexual perversion – necrophilia. His victims were two prepubescent females and one pubescent female."

He paused for effect. The doctors looked at each other.

"He is delusional and believes Greek mythology is true. When people react to his claim with humor, he sees them as idiots. Eddie is watching over Riley's adjustment to our hospital. We'll give him some time with the patient and make a diagnostic assessment in a few months."

Turning to Dr. Brenner, he added, "Mr. Eddie Fisk is a patient attendant who has been with us for several years. His work load has been expanded to address unique cases. Frankly, there are times when we find him indispensable."

Dr. Reed moved his eyes over the faces looking at him.

"Any questions?"

Dr. Brenner considered asking Dr. Reed about the expected prognosis of Mr. Riley Nacht, but then decided to hold his tongue. Recalling his days at Cherokee State Hospital, where he had a violent murderer in their facility, who died in a scuffle with another patient. He thought it better his colleagues not know.

"If there's nothing else, we'll adjourn."

Squeak of chairs being dragged against the tiled floor filled the room, as the physician's prepared to leave the office and start their day.

* * *

The next morning, Eddie went to visit Riley before breakfast. The idea being to catch Riley at different times of the day to throw off his rhythm. It would not take long for him to realize Eddie's position of power. And Riley was all about power.

When Eddie approached Riley's cell, he found him towel-drying his face over the sink. Eddie watched Riley finish and turn around.

"Good morning."

Riley ignored him.

"So, tell me about the universe, the sun, the moon, the planets." Eddie crossed his arms in front and stood with legs shoulder-width apart.

"Why should I?"

"You don't have to. It might pass the time."

Riley folded the towel and placed it on the edge of the sink. He walked two steps to the table and chair, turned the chair around to face Eddie and sat down.

"I'd offer you a seat, but you can see my accommodations are lacking." He scratched the side of his face, the stubble itching him.

Shaving was a challenge in a maximum-security environment because the razor could be used in depraved ways. In Riley's case, protocol required he wear a straight-jacket, which he would don, turn his back to the bars and the straps on the apparatus tied. Once secured, a guard could open the barred-door of his cell so that another person could shave Riley's face at the sink. A guard stood at the door watching. Riley got a shave once a week. It helped keep the lice down.

Eddie leaned against the far wall near Riley's cell still crossing his arms.

Riley needs a shave soon.

"Astronomy studies the cyclical position of our solar system that includes the sun, moons, planets and stars. At the watch factory, I used the planets and the stars in our solar system to set the accuracy of Elgin timing devises."

"I didn't know about that."

"What? That I worked at the factory?"

"No. I didn't know clock precision was set by the stars."

"Have you ever noticed the building with the dome at the Elgin factory?"

"Yeah."

"That's where the telescope is."

"Huh. So, how many planets are there?" asked Eddie interested.

"Nine. Using our sun as a reference, the planets are Mercury, Venus, Earth, Mars, Jupiter, Saturn, Uranus, Neptune and Pluto. There are other suns in the universe, other solar systems. Generally, when we build better telescopes, we make more discoveries. The University of Chicago has telescopes in different areas in Illinois."

"Is that where you graduated?"

"Yes. You see, that's why astronomy is exciting. It's unraveling how the gods played."

"You talked about the god's yesterday."

"I talked about their supreme power yesterday," Riley corrected him. "I didn't talk about the gods themselves. "

"Will you talk about them now?"

"No. But I will tell you more about their essence. How they came to be. How I know them, their stories. The stories are true and I see their truth in the stars."

Eddie intrigued. "Can you predict?"

Riley did not answer. Instead, he smiled, as if from a secret closely held, with eyes of a soulless entity peeking through their orbital windows. A shiver slid down Eddie's spine as he flexed the long fingers of his left hand to ward off the chill. A moment passed.

Eddie broke the silence.

"Well, I wish I could talk more, but I have things to do. Have a nice day."

Riley didn't respond.

As usual, Eddie had a busy itinerary. A new patient needed admission; male, twenty-five years old, paralyzed from the waist down. Fortunately, he did well using his wheel chair and could get around almost entirely on his own. His paralysis could not be medically explained, which was why he was being admitted to the mental hospital.

* * *

This malady would later be called "conversion paralysis". One possible explanation is an unresolved conflict within the patient such that the negative energy (i.e. anxiety) is reflected in a physical response.

* * *

Next, he had to check on the patients in the male dormitory and enter his observations on his daily report. One man, in delirium tremens, needed periodic checks to avoid patient disturbances, in case a violent alcoholic seizure overwhelmed him. Eddie gazed at the sweaty man floating in and out of consciousness.

No good bum. Do us a favor and die. Get it over with.

And sometime during the day, the hospital needed Eddie to transport a recently deceased woman to the hospital morgue. No hurry, but it needed to be done before six o'clock.

When Eddie reported his talk with Riley. Dr. Reed scratched his temple and asked, "Is that what he said exactly? 'It's unraveling how the Gods played'?"

"Yes, Sir."

"That's interesting. You got into his head a bit. Good job, Eddie. Keep at it."

CHAPTER TWENTY-FOUR
Constellatio
1926

Eddie, sitting on the floor with his back to the wall made sure he was out of Riley's reach. He listened to Riley with rapt attention.

"Her name is, Persephone, a goddess of the spring. Her mother, Demeter, the harvest goddess, and her father, Zeus, the god supreme. Persephone is well-formed, beautiful. Hades wanted her, desired her. She had walked along a garden on a spring day and bent down to pick a flower. Hades opened the ground beneath and raped her on the spot, before he abducted her to his kingdom in hell."

Riley was sitting on a wooden chair looking at Eddie. He turned briefly gesturing to the window built high up on the far wall. He could barely make out the spring season, soft green grass appearing like a wink of an eye through the window pane.

"Zeus implored Hades to return the lovely Persephone and he complied, but not before tricking Persephone into eating pomegranate seeds, the food of the underworld. Eventually released, Persephone returned to the land of the gods and goddesses, but spent the winter months with her husband, Hades."

"Is this story reflected in the stars?"

Riley got up from his chair next to the table and walked toward Eddie. He crossed is arms.

"Yes. It's reflected in the constellation Virgo, which appears in the Northern Hemisphere in the spring. One can see Demeter holding a sheaf of corn."

Riley broke a pregnant pause.

"Have you ever heard of astrology?"

Eddie shook his head.

"Astrology is used to describe human characteristics, personalities. In fact, some people are astrologically compatible, others are not."

"Are you astrologically compatible with anyone?" asked Eddie.

Riley would not answer his question.

"You see Virgo's are very precise. They wonder, explore. They like to learn and compete. They tend to have scholastic achievement. They find it frustrating to bow down to acceptable social mores, knowing that not doing so causes residual difficulties. And so, they comply to avoid distractions. However, a true virgo-ian, if there was a such a word, knows how to manipulate events, for discretionary purposes, in the social arena, while they pursue their own prerogatives."

Riley waited, thinking.

"It sounds like they may be critical of other people," Eddie finally said.

Riley's eyebrows went up, surprised. "Yes, they tend to be critical. It's part of their analytical slant."

Eddie shifted his position off the floor, lifting himself to stand. "You are a Virgo, aren't you?"

"Yes, I am. And you, Eddie, are a Sagittarius."

"I am?" Eddie raised his brows.

"You tell me. When is your birthday?"

"December third."

"Of course. The Centaur, half-man and half-horse, hunting with bow drawn."

Eddie, uncomfortable, wondered if he had made a mistake. Riley had deftly shifted the focus of their discussion.

Riley continued. "You're restless. There are times when you operate blindly, which often leads to risk-taking, and sometimes, cynicism. You have a good work ethic and a strong sense of duty. You long for a period where you can shirk responsibility and be carefree."

"That can apply to anyone," Eddie said defensively.

Riley kept on. "Being half-horse and half-man, you find it difficult to find acceptance. At best, what you get is tolerance. What you really want is love; a mature love, so sometimes you act out in frustration."

"Now that's enough," Eddie replied, a flush throughout his body. "I have other things to do, so I'll see you later."

Riley saw the pain in Eddie's face as Eddie walked away. When he heard the heavy prison door close, he sighed and turned toward a half-read book lying on the table top in his cell.

Eddie's afternoon was devoted to supervising five adolescent male patients to thoroughly clean the communal kitchen.

Now in a nasty mood, Eddie was cross with one kid, who couldn't seem to get the hang of mopping a floor. After whacking him on his head, Eddie had the boy stand in the corner of the room with his nose pressed to the wall. He ignored muffled sounds of tears and watched as the other boys cleaned their assignments with more energy.

Afterwards, when all the patients had been delivered to their assigned dormitories, Eddie headed toward Dr. Reed's office.

He had trouble reporting his conversation with Riley to Dr. Reed that day. Too much information with subjects unfamiliar to him. Mythology, astronomy, and something new he had never heard – astrology? All so confusing.

"We talked about mythology, Persephone, in particular."

"Now, that's interesting. How is Persephone connected to the stars?"

Eddie felt embarrassed not recalling the details. "If I remember what he told me, it's through Persephone's mother. She's displayed in the constellation Virgo."

"Ahhh," Dr. Reed mused. "Her name is Demeter, right?"

"Yes, that's right!" Eddie exclaimed, surprised. "But there is more. He said I am a Sagittarius and told me things about me."

I see what's happening here. Riley is bringing him into his world. I better watch that he's not taking control. Maybe I better have him report to me every time he talks to Riley. Keep an eye on things.

"It sounds like he knows things he learned in college. Greek mythology. Astrology is nothing but a prostituted version of Greek and Roman mythology, with some spirituality sprinkled in."

Eddie nodded.

"Did this bother you? Do you want to stop talking to him?"

Eddie answered truthfully. "I'd like to keep going with this, if that's okay with you, Sir. I want this experience."

"Well, okay. Let's discuss your conversations with him, shall we?"

Eddie nodded. "I appreciate that, Doctor."

Dr. Riley wanted to reassure him. "I think you're doing fine. Pretty soon, though, I want to spend some time with him myself."

"Of course."

"Thank you, Eddie. And let me know if there are any other concerns."

"Concerns? Like what?"

Dr. Riley noticed Eddie's posture changed with a hard expression.

Ouch. I may have gone too far...ego...

"Nothing in particular. Just anything that may come up."

Riley's face softened. "To be honest, Sir, it might help if I read about Riley's subjects. I won't be an expert. It'd just help me if I knew something about astronomy and mythology."

"Good point, Eddie. Okay, let's do that. I'll call the library at the University of Chicago and arrange your visit there."

"Thank you, Sir!"

"You do a good job, Eddie. When you are doing special work like this, it makes sense to give you some help."

When he left Dr. Reed's office, Eddie felt elated, determined to succeed.

Dr. Reed noticed my work. Maybe there is a promotion in store, possible college opportunity – who knows what's around the corner?

A few days later, Eddie drove to the Chicago North Shore and Milwaukee Railroad to take the North Shore Line to Chicago. Then he used the trolley car system to make his way to the University of Chicago. Once there, he found the Harper Memorial Library.

He found the university grounds to be intimidating, particularly the library in gothic architecture, rectangle with two structures at either end that resembled rook pieces on a chess board.

Glad I wore my Sunday best suit. Damn. I forgot to have the left coat sleeve lengthened.

Always an irritating issue, having his clothes adjusted for his body.

Too busy to have it tailored and I keep forgetting. Don't wear it often enough, I guess.

He made his way up the concrete steps, through the double doors, and walked to the receptionist desk. A small woman, brown hair pulled back tight in a bun, looked at Eddie through her heavy- rimmed glasses.

Bug-eyed Betty.

She wore a simple, long-sleeved black dress with a white lace collar too severe for her features.

"May I help you?" she whispered.

"Yes, thank you," he spoke softly. "I'm Mr. Fisk. Dr. Reed arranged for my visit. I'd like to peruse books on Greek mythology and astronomy." He paused, not sure to ask this, "And... do you have a book on astrology?"

He expected her to react negatively to this question, knowing astrology was looked down upon by Dr. Reed. Instead, he was surprised when she did not react at all. He watched as she took a piece of paper and wrote the locations of books on mythology, astronomy, and astrology.

"Here you go," she said as she handed him the paper and pointed. "You'll find these books on the ground floor to the right."

"Thank you."

The ceiling height, two stories tall. The resulting acoustics made it difficult for Eddie to walk quietly to the book shelves. It bothered him to be mindful of his movements, but after he chose a few books, he found a table where he could sit comfortably and began to read. Now, he found the silence to be a benefactor to concentration as he delved deep into uncharted territory.

CHAPTER TWENTY-FIVE

Zeus

1927

For a few moths Eddie often thought of what he had read about Greek mythology. It affected the way he viewed female patients and nurses.

Persephone must be blond. The sort of blond hair that's platinum. And marble white skin. Pure and sexy. Polar opposites to Hades. Disturbing.

The thought of her struck him too deeply; familiar and strange. He let out a deep sigh and shook himself back into reality.

Occasionally Demeter came to mind. He could see her in his mother. It was the way she cared for him. Nurturing.

But Athena, too strong, could never submit to a mate, remained a virgin.

Interesting she had no mate. I wonder if she ever felt longing?

It was a discussion in his head that popped up intermittently when his path crossed a woman at the hospital.

Too much time had lapsed since his last visit with Riley.

"Hello, Riley." Eddie had his hands in the pockets of his taupe pants. He wore a white shirt with his sleeves rolled up above his elbows. The top of his shirt was unbuttoned so Riley could see Eddie had been sweating. The heaviness of Eddie's beard, even though shaven that morning, collected small droplets of sweat.

Riley was sitting on his bed, reading a book. He wore boxer underpants and a T-shirt. He too had been sweating.

Riley's face is clean shaven. Nice.

"Where have you been?"

"Too much work to do." Eddie shrugged.

"Tell me about your work; maybe something about the patients here."

Eddie didn't take the bait.

"How about you tell me about Zeus."

"Ah, you've been reading about mythology."

"A little bit."

"I'm flattered. Really! Well..." Riley put his book down, rose from the bed and walked to the chair set by the table. Placing his hands on the chairback, he leaned on it until the front chair legs hovered inches above the floor.

"The god of the gods, Zeus. All other gods deferred to him. Ultimate power and authority."

"But how did it all start?"

"It started out of love from dear Mother Earth, and with the dawning of earth came the heavens, the universe, and the gods."

Eddie thought of his mother again, the way he felt about her nurturing love, powerful and safe.

"So, that's the mythological view. What is the view from astronomy?"

Riley chuckled with delight.

*He **has** been reading.*

"It's called the 'Big Bang Theory'. You see, we weren't there, so we have to hypothesize and draw upon what we know about the gods. A man named Lemaître thinks the universe came from a single atom. That's an intriguing notion, don't you think? It's possible it was a massive blast of energy; whose source is unknown. It's possible that energy might have come from a single atom. The problem is we simply get a view of the universe in the middle of time, not knowing with surety the conditions proceeding the big-bang event, assuming big-bang is true."

"Do you believe it is true?"

"Yes."

"Why?"

"Because there are too many similarities between mythological events and scientific events. Statistical probability weighs in that direction. Moreover, the myths come from ancient sources who, I believe, were wise before our time. We don't know how they became wise. We only know wisdom took place."

Eddie sucked in his breath.

"So, who came before Zeus?"

"Zeus's father is Cronus, the Greek Titan God of Time."

"Amazing."

"Yes, it is amazing. I appreciate you seeing it that way, because the fourth dimension is time."

"What?" Eddie raised his eyebrows.

"Yes, three-dimensional space: width, length, height. The fourth dimension is time," Riley explained.

"Of course."

"To be more accurate, Einstein called it '*spacetime*'. It considers the point of view of the observer at a point in time."

Eddie was intrigued now. "I remember reading a bit about Einstein, but I've never studied him."

"Sounds like you missed out, but that's okay. If you'd like, I could teach you a few things."

Eddie considered this proposal. *This is probably okay. Dr. Reed wants me to spend time with him. Yes.*

"Yeah, I'd like that."

"And maybe you can tell me about your patients?"

"Why do you want to know?"

"Boredom. I'd like to know what your work is like, your patients."

I don't see the harm.

"Okay. Sorry, but I have to go."

"Will you be back tomorrow?" Riley asked.

"I'll try. It depends what happens during the day."

A surge of adrenalin rushed through Riley's body in anticipation. Respiration increased. He stayed silent as he watched Eddie turn away and disappear. His eyes glazed over momentarily; revealing an unobserved hint of madness.

CHAPTER TWENTY-SIX
Scary Movie Night
1927

Christmas season. Roache Boarding School temporarily closed, with students spending time with their families.

She knocked gently on her father's office door.

"Come in, Kimberly."

Opening the door, Kimberly paused in the doorway, hand still on the doorknob.

Kimberly was twelve-years-old now, almost an adult by Warren's eyes. He sometimes looked upon his daughter with amazement, considering her striking resemblance to her mother, Lucinda. She had Lucinda's mannerisms, her voice. Kimberly's developing breasts had become more apparent, too.

Thank God Miss Oberson helped Kimberly buy her first undergarment. Sending Kimberly to boarding school was the best thing I did.

"Father, may I go to a movie with Carolyn tonight?"

"Pastor Tallent's daughter?"

She nodded.

"What movie?"

"It's called '*London After Midnight*'."

"Who's taking you?"

"Will you ask William to drive us?"

"Well, okay. Come home directly after the movie."

"Yes, Father, after we take Carolyn home."

"Fine. That's fine," he replied absentmindedly, looking at a paper he was holding.

An afterthought. He raised his eyes to his daughter. "And tell me about the movie tomorrow at our Christmas Eve breakfast."

She giggled. "I will, Father." Then backed out, closing the door.

Kimberly called Carolyn from the drawing room.

"Father said 'yes'. Did your father say you can go?"

"Yes."

"Wonderful! What are you going to wear?"

"I thought I'd wear a black dress."

"The new one? Long sleeves? Velvet?"

"Uh-huh."

"I'll wear my black one, too. It's satin and lace. What about jewelry?"

"My father doesn't like me to wear jewelry."

Kimberly knew about Pastor Tallent's conservative views.

"Neither does my father, but put something in your purse. You can put it on while William drives us."

Carolyn giggled. "Good idea. It's cold, so we'll need coats."

"And hats and gloves!" Kimberly added. "So, William and I will pick you up at five-thirty for the six o'clock show. I'll send William to buy our tickets early."

"Okay. This'll be fun. See you then!"

Hours later, William was driving Miss Kimberly and Miss Carolyn to the movie house in the Weatherspoon's navy-blue Whippet Model Sedan. The girls giggled while they adorned themselves with parental contraband – jewelry, lipstick and perfume. William pretended not to notice.

When William parked the car next to the sidewalk, he and Kimberly synchronized their Elgin-made watches and confirmed the time he was to pick them up later. Meanwhile, passers-by paused our slowed their sidewalk stroll to view the luxurious navy-blue sedan.

Nifty!

Tickets in hand, the girls nearly ran to the door of the movie house. They almost knocked a man down. Kimberly paused and apologized to the stranger, in his twenties, noticing his awkward shoulder that tilted his body, and a left hand with fingers too long. It was almost dark outside and she shivered, not knowing if it was the nighttime chill or the stranger she had encountered.

Eddie, caught off guard, glanced at the females, then at the sedan being driven away, and back to the blond hastily entering the building. *That doll's gotta have a daddy.*

He moved to the movie line to purchase a ticket. A couple in front of him were holding hands.

Love birds. Eddie sighed, wishing he had a date.

The girls found their seats in the center near the front, settled themselves in and chatted in low tones, mimicking adult behavior. As the movie progressed, their prepubescent nature became apparent to their neighbors. They cringed with the words "*...they're dead people from the grave. Vampires...!*" And when Lon Chaney performed his bat-pose, with knife-like teeth and insane eyes, the girls barely refrained from screaming, biting down on clenched knuckles. A flatulent response became apparent to those sitting nearby.

A dark story – suicide? Not so. The truth wrangled out by a hypnotist – eyes riveting with power. "*...please don't ask me...*", a suspect cries out. The trances! A way for the hypnotist to re-enact the sinful crime and ferret out the culprit.

The girls squirmed with the urgency to pee. Sitting two rows behind the girls and to the side, Eddie caught their reaction and laughed out loud.

When the movie finally ended, the badly shaken girls collected themselves, huddling together in whispers.

"Are there such things as Vampires?" Carolyn asked.

"No. It's just a story."

"How about hypnotism? Do you think that's real?"

"Yes, I think it is."

"That was a scary movie!"

Kimberly nodded. "Let's find William. I'm sure he's waiting outside for us."

He was.

Eddie watched the girls slip into the automobile. *I wonder if that bucket's bent?*

Then, he walked on, hands in his pockets, coat collar curled up as the Whippet sped away. Somehow, thinking the car was stolen made him feel better.

Kimberly had trouble getting to sleep when she finally went to bed. She tossed and turned remembering scenes of Lon Chaney as Inspector Edward C. Burke – the hypnotist.

When someone else – something evil – has power over you... I don't think I could endure.

Chills ran down her back and would not stop, even though her bed was warm. She felt cramps in her abdomen. A combination of sweat and cold.

Do I have the flu?

At one point she rose from her bed and looked out through the window. It was a dark night of a new moon. She used the bathroom and went back to bed. Finally, sleep overtook her. When she woke early, she was startled to see blood-stained sheets made by her first period.

Oh, no! I left Miss Oberson's box at the school!

After wiping herself clean, she placed some folded tissues inside her panties for a makeshift pad. Then donning her bathrobe and bedroom slippers, she tiptoed to the kitchen where she hoped to find William. Thankfully, he was there.

She noticed her father had not yet risen for the day.

"Pssst, William, come over here," she gestured, standing in the alcove next to the door leading to the kitchen and coat closets, the door under the winding staircase. She didn't want the cook to hear their conversation, because he was male and she was too embarrassed for him to know.

"Yes, Miss Kimberly?"

"I need you to run to the store and buy me a box of Kotex. I've started." She blushed.

William, embarrassed and nervous, retrieved a hanky from the inside of his topcoat and began to wipe his wide brow, his hairline receding. "Oh, no, Miss Kimberly. Please don't ask me to do that."

"William, I can't do this myself," she whispered. "There is no woman here for me to ask. You know things about my dad and me. We trust you. It's as if you're family. I can't do this by myself."

"You need a woman to do this," he whispered.

"Who do you suggest?" She lifted her shoulders and her hands, palms up, her eyes wide.

"How about Carolyn's mother?"

"Oh! That's a good idea!" She started to relax. "I'll call her now. Thank you for thinking of that. I could give you a hug!"

"Oh, *no*, Miss Kimberly. Please don't do that. It's *so* inappropriate." William clutched his left arm against his torso, his right hand on his cheek. A barrier.

Kimberly giggled, hiding her smile behind her hand. "Thank you, William. Will you please tell my father I'm not feeling well? I won't be having breakfast with him."

"Of course, but you need to eat. I'll serve your eggs and toast in an hour, upstairs in your room, okay?"

"Thank you." Her lower lip went forward in a pretty pout.

"And when Carolyn's mother delivers your...ahem... package, I'll deliver it to your room immediately."

"I don't know what I would do without you, William."

They parted with William returning to the kitchen and Kimberly upstairs to her room.

She called Carolyn's mother, Mrs. Tallent, and explained her plight. An hour later, Mrs. Tallent went inside a drug store with bag in hand, found the necessary items, placed the money in the money jar nearby, put the items in her bag and exited the store.

It was all so *"hush hush"*. Social decorum insisted the word "Kotex" never be used in public. Propriety created a mechanism where the purchase of Kotex and belt was made discreet by the use of a special money box. This protected the privacy of female customers who never, ever discussed such delicate matters in public, in mixed company, or at a cash register.

* * *

A soft knock at Mr. Weatherspoon's bedroom door.

"Mr. Weatherspoon, it's William."

"Just a moment." Then, "Come in."

The butler entered the room keeping his eyes on his master. He knew a woman had spent the night with Mr. Weatherspoon, but it was his duty, as a servant, to refrain from making this knowledge obvious. He addressed Warren as if she was not there.

Warren and the woman had donned bathrobes and slippers and were standing in the middle of the room. The bed behind them in disarray.

"Sir, you need to be aware of recent events regarding Kimberly."

"Oh?"

A clearing of his throat. "Yes, Sir." A pause. "It seems your child is no longer a child. She is now a woman."

"What do you mean?" Warren asked.

"She's started, Sir." William looked uncomfortable.

Warren's eyes furrowed, questioning. "Started what?"

The woman laughed, her presence now officially recognized by her indiscretion. William looked at her pleadingly, and then tried again. "A gift from mother nature."

The woman contributed, "A visit from Aunt Flo. Lady business."

In an expression of recognition, Warren lifted his eyebrows, looked at the woman, and then at William. "Well, well. Is that so?"

Relieved, William explained, "Kimberly asks to have her breakfast in her room, since she's not feeling well."

Warren smiled at his butler. "Thank you, William. Will you please check on her throughout the day?"

"Of course. You need to know she has called Carolyn's mother to provide her with the necessary articles she now needs."

Warren nodded. "Thank you for telling me."

Looking at the woman, Warren said, "I have to start the day, my dear. William will help you leave."

She gathered the silk robe around her ample bosom, crossing her arms in front. The robe, too large, gathered around her bare feet. "Please, give me thirty minutes," she said to William.

"Of course." William stepped back to the doorway and whispered, "In thirty minutes, I'll show you the back way."

He closed the door.

CHAPTER TWENTY-SEVEN
Quaesto
1927

"So, tell me about the movie..." Riley lay out-stretched on his cot, his arms behind his head and his feet crossed.

Eddie glanced at the window high up, near the ceiling, to view grass and gray sky. He felt sorry for Riley being locked up in his cell for over two years now.

He can't even enjoy fresh air.

He turned his eyes to Riley. There was black dirt on the bottoms of his feet.

"It was scary to most folks, but not to me. A wealthy man died by suicide and his mansion became inhabited by ghouls and vampires. Lon Chaney's vampire teeth made some scenes memorable."

Riley chuckled as Eddie continued.

"Oh, it's a great flick for a guy to take a girl. She gets scared and the guy can put his arm around her."

"What's it called?"

"'*London After Midnight*'...at the end, the man gets the girl after they figure out it wasn't suicide but a murder. The inspector has the gift of inducing trances to those he wanted to question. Those scenes were potent."

"Hypnotic trances?" asked Riley.

"Yep. His influential power. The inspector used this to bring on an altered state of consciousness."

Surprise. A simple conversation, relaxed, going nowhere, and suddenly a change in Riley's countenance as he responded to the phrase, "an altered state of consciousness." Somnambulistic.

The hair on Eddie's arms stood on end as he watched Riley slowly shift himself up in his cot, swinging his knees around so that his feet touched the floor, and then walked toward Eddie. Eddie stepped back, putting distance between him and the jail bars. He waited for Riley to say something.

"That's it! It's magnetism. Electromagnetism. Of course!"

Riley began to pace the width of his cell along the bars. Eddie observed his pondering, paralyzed by the excitement and agitated muttering.

Is this Riley speaking? Or is it something that has Riley – a spirit?

"Electromagnetism is part of life, part of the molecular chemistry. Weak forces and strong forces. I missed it because it's so small and the universe is…" He stopped for a moment. "Weak forces and strong forces. Weak forces and strong forces. It's…it's transformational. That fundamental molecular elements can be changed. We see this all the time. The forces are the gods."

Riley stopped pacing. Stopped muttering. He stood there for a moment, thoughts racing.

"I don't know how gravitational pull fits in. I know there is more. Much more. It's beyond anything."

Eddie still stood there, rapt.

Then, Riley's eyes met Eddie's.

"It goes to stars and galaxies and atoms and molecules. Infinity. Interactions, both weak and strong, small and large – very large. Cosmic forces."

Riley then looked away from Eddie and around him, his circumstances, his cell, and he started to weep.

Eddie waited patiently as Riley sobbed out gibberish. His body trembled. His hands covered his face. Eventually, he regained lucidity, sighed deeply, wiped his eyes with the end of his T-shirt and his hands on the bottom of his shorts.

I gotta get out of here.

"Well," he said, "it was just a thought." He turned away and lay back down on his bed, turning to the cell wall, hiding his face.

Eddie said nothing. He glanced again at the bottom of Eddie's feet, darkened by the dust and grime on the cell floor.

* * *

Later that evening, Eddie told Dr. Reed what had happened. Dr. Reed thanked Eddie before he left his office, and then reconsidered what to do with Mr. Riley Nacht.

An episode. Surprised it took this long to occur. Not sure we can help him.

I wonder if we have an opportunity here to look at other disciplines besides psychiatry. Research. Potential psychiatric doctors and PhD's looking for thesis subjects.

Let's see. How about phrenology, for instance. And criminology, psychology, degeneration theory...and perhaps...anthropological criminology. I wonder if Riley would be of interest to our universities for research purposes. I wonder if we could get financial compensation for his care from these sources. I wonder if, rather than having a costly liability in our midst, that instead we have a potential opportunity.

The next morning, Dr. Reed drafted a letter.

[Date]
[University Name]
[University Department]
[University Address]

[University Phone Number]
Dear [Department Head Name],

As Superintendent of Elgin State Mental Hospital, I propose a unique opportunity I believe will be of interest to you. We have a criminal psychopathic patient who demonstrates singular characteristics. It is my understanding your institution may be interested in this patient for use of research or study in a discipline you may see fit.

If this idea appeals to you, please respond so we can further discuss an arrangement. I will provide more details of the patient's description and behavior at that time. Together, we can determine if there is a mutually agreeable contract that serves us both, as well as the welfare of the patient.

Sincerely,

Dr. Reed, Superintendent of Elgin State Mental Hospital
Elgin State Mental Hospital
Elgin, Illinois
Phone Number: Elgin 8437

Satisfied, Dr. Reed left his office and headed downstairs to his secretary's desk where he found her typing.

"Stephanie," he said, as he handed her his handwritten scribble, "please type this up by the end of the day and make ten copies."

Stephanie perused the paper he handed her.

"What are the brackets for?" she asked.

"I intend to send this letter, with changes, to several institutions. It's basically the same letter, but there will be modifications depending upon to whom this letter is sent."

"I'll be happy to type this up, it won't take long. Instead of making ten copies, why don't I make one copy today for you to look over. Meanwhile, give me a list of the institutions you want to contact and

I'll get the addresses, phone numbers and contact names. Then you can review and approve each letter before I send it out."

"Thank you, Stephanie. I don't know what I would do without you."

Stephanie smiled back at Dr. Reed as she placed the paper next to her typewriter and continued her work.

The strategy worked. Some responses came by phone, others by letters.

September 5, 1927
Dear Dr. Nigel Reed,

I truly appreciate your thoughtfulness in sending your proposal to our university. While phrenology has been an interest in the past, the discipline has evolved into the study of physiognomy, which is in keeping with our current interest in eugenics. Is your subject a male member of an inferior race (not Caucasian)? If so, we would like to participate in a study of your patient. We have a PhD-bound candidate, who is comparing skulls and brains of ethnic groups in an effort to determine a ranking of races that is part of evolution. The study is currently limited to males, since females tend to have an underdeveloped cranial system and are therefore not within the scope of our interests.

We recognize the singular opportunity you propose, given your subject has already been diagnosed as a severe psychopath. This, by itself, offers a basis of comparison to healthier-functioning brains.

Please give me a call so we can discuss this more thoroughly.

Very Truly Yours...

* * *

January 16, 1928
Dear Dr. Nigel Reed,

    My name is Victor Lewrenski. I am a student at Georgetown University working on a doctoral thesis in Criminal Anthropology. I am working on a hypothesis that a crime event is closely related to the personality, mental capacity and physical appearance of the criminal.

    It has been brought to my attention that you have opened your doors for a student such as me to study a criminal psychopath presently residing at Elgin State Mental Hospital. I am in a position to compensate you whether it be financial, as a recognized contributor to my research or both...

* * *

April 27, 1930
Dear Dr. Nigel Reed,

    I was reminded by the Department Head of Psychology at the University of Michigan of your offer to make available a criminal psychopath for academic study purposes. I am a student at Michigan who would like to spend time interviewing your patient. I believe his name is Mr. Riley Nacht. Is he still residing at Elgin State Mental Hospital? If so, please contact me for a discussion on this matter. I will be happy to compensate you...

* * *

March 3, 1931
Dear Dr. Nigel Reed,

    I am a criminologist working for the State of Maryland who is interested in field work and fact-finding endeavors in crimes of moral turpitude. I talked to Chief Sonne on this matter and he gave me your name, contact information and told me about the criminal psychopath I believe is still living at Elgin State Mental Hospital. I would like interview this man for research purposes.

Please let me know your terms of agreement ...

* * *

April 10, 1931
Dear Mr. Nigel Reed,

I am a student of psychology and sexology studying the works of Dr. Havelock Ellis. I am very interested in interviewing a patient of yours, Mr. Riley Nacht. Imagine my interest in this man's behavior, a unique sexual deviant. Please let me know if I can arrange some time talking with him...

* * *

Over time Dr. Reed used his contacts with universities and his influence within the medical and law enforcement communities to provide financial compensation for the hospital's care of Riley. At first Riley was annoyed, but later came to appreciate the attention. When visits became onerous, he shut down. Dr. Read realized Riley was never a social person and tended toward isolation. It occurred to him these visits could produce an event that could put the hospital and the patient in jeopardy. The program was cancelled.

CHAPTER TWENTY-EIGHT
Immanis (Enormous)
1927

Dr. Reed, sitting in his office for privacy, reflected upon the many events unfolding at the hospital these last few years. Unprecedented population growth, primarily due to WWI veterans, endlessly seeking help. Fortunately, their services were funded by the U.S. government and the State of Illinois.

But there were other patients, too – a growing geriatric population, females and children with mental illnesses.

How do you teach mentally ill children? How do you prepare them for life?

A deep sigh as he pondered debilitating patient volume, considering the *'want-to-have'* desires and the *'need-to-have'* requirements. It all came down to new facilities; building construction always in full swing. Relentless.

Elgin State Mental Hospital must be as self-sufficient as possible – grow our own food, slaughter our own meat, use the backbone of some of our patients. That will work in the long run. It would be less expensive, therapeutic, and develop needed skills and training while we also cure.

But it didn't stop there. Dr. Reed had other aspirations.

I want to see a new building that would house research, experiments and chemicals using shock therapy. Shock therapy has so much to offer.

He sighed imagining professional acclaim and personal satisfaction.

Build to put ourselves out of business. How ironic is that!

He glanced up at door after hearing a knock.

"Come in."

It was Eddie. The doctor saw the strain on his face outlined by the heavy stubble of beard he knew so well.

"Long day? Sit down, Eddie." Dr. Reed gestured to the chair.

"Thank you."

Eddie walked to the chair in front of his desk and sat down, while the doctor swiveled his chair to the side, stretching his legs.

"How are things going with Riley?"

"Honestly, Sir, I don't know if what I am doing is helpful."

"Tell me about your last talk with him."

"Sure. We talked about Zeus and the fourth dimension, time. I admit it has been a while since I've spent time with him. My schedule doesn't always allow it. You know the man has a simple family story. His family came from Germany before WWI. There's not that much to tell."

"There is more going on than you realize, Eddie." Dr. Reed fiddled with his pipe, his elbows on the top of his desk. "You are both only children and male. You two have a common background in growing up. This is one reason why I chose you to work with him. I assumed you would like seeing the criminal mind at work – the psychopathic mind."

"That's right. I like the work. I just don't see the point of it." Eddie scratched his chin.

"Consider it research. There's little expectation that Riley Nacht will become an outstanding member of society."

Eddie laughed and relaxed.

"What we have here is an opportunity to research how his mind works, figure out the moment when he is provoked into criminal action."

Eddie risked annoying the doctor. "Frankly, Dr. Reed, it might be time for you to talk with him."

Dr. Reed consider his words.

The time. How can I spend time on something that cannot heal? Eddie is right. I need to steer this ship better.

"Alright, Eddie. I'll come with you tomorrow morning and we'll both have a chat with Mr. Riley Nacht."

That night, before Dr. Reed went to bed, he re-considered his talk with Eddie about Riley Nacht.

I had hoped Eddie would take more initiative. He does what I ask him, but nothing more. I'm disappointed he does not demonstrate drive. He could be doing some research himself. Instead, I have to push him into action. He is not the leader I hoped for. It is what it is.

The next morning, Dr. Reed and Eddie were standing close to Riley's cell, but being cautious to stay out of reach. Riley was eating his breakfast off a metal tray, the kind used in the military.

"Good morning," Dr. Reed said.

Riley took a spoonful of porridge and looked at Dr. Reed, nodding while chewing. He was wearing underwear, T-shirt, and the boxer shorts he had slept in.

"Mind if we have a chat?"

He swallowed, sat back and paused for a moment in thought, then ignored Dr. Reed and focused on his meal.

"I want to ask you about the murders."

Riley hunched down further over his tray and concentrated on his food.

After seeing his reaction, Dr. Reed had an idea. "The stars are at their brightest on nights of a new moon. When you killed Dorothy, you were watching Orion, right?"

Riley swallowed, put down his spoon and wiped his mouth across his forearm. He then shoved his chair back from the table, crossed his arms, and stretched his legs out, crossing them at his ankles.

"I didn't murder anyone. 'Murder' is a bad word. It implies something wrong, immoral. I did nothing wrong. I had the right to hunt."

"Who gave you the right?"

He glared at Dr. Reed.

Eddie watched Riley's demeanor change, becoming hardened, intense. Eddie felt a shiver down his back once more.

"Cronus."

Dr. Reed racked his memory to recall the god, Cronus. "It was time," he finally said.

Riley gave him a contemptuous smile.

"Ah…" Dr. Reed nodded. He realized Riley spoke of 'time' in two ways: in terms of '*action*', and of '*the right moment*'.

"Is this true of…" Dr. Reed hesitated as he looked for the right words. Not finding them, he rephrased. "This is true of the others."

Riley gave a slight nod of his head indicating his appreciation for the doctor's grasp of these things.

The doctor looked down and let his focus concentrate on the spot where the cell bars attached to a rail that was fastened to the floor by screws in the cement. It wasn't the rail that interested him. He simply disengaged from Riley for a moment while he negotiated in his mind.

Hunters dismember their kill. I understand that. But where does the necrophilia come from? Most likely from fear of rejection. The dead cannot respond. Now I think I understand. There's more to his dismemberment of bodies. It's sexual, like a fetish. And he's exploring this fetish, which explains why his crimes escalated.

Riley and Eddie watched the doctor think – kicking ideas around. Moments passed before Dr. Reed raised his eyes to Riley again.

"Mr. Nacht, I'm going to try to help you as best I can, but it may take a long time."

"The only help I want, Doctor, is to go home. Can you do that?"

"I can't promise. We'll see how things go."

Riley lunged forward, grasping the seat with his hands, then scooted the chair closer to his table and resumed eating. Dismissal.

Dr. Reed gave him a final look, then turned and walked down the hall, Eddie silently following.

The doctor considered Riley's energy, like an aura around him, that made him think of Caligula, the old Roman Emperor of ancient history, believed to have been insane.

It's said Caligula had epilepsy, that his epileptic attacks were associated with the full moon. Riley's murders are associated with the moon. What else? There's something else... that Caligula cut out his baby from his sister, Drusilla. Incest. Tried to re-enact the birth of Athena. Riley is obsessed with mythology, too. There are too many associations here. Cutting. Blood. The gods. Fascinating, all the congruencies.

CHAPTER TWENTY-NINE

Ricky Esposito

1931

Milwaukee Avenue was a major highway running north and south through downtown Libertyville, Illinois. It boasted a variety of stores, mostly two-storied buildings, circa 1920s. At one time these were row-houses. Eventually, the bottom floor became the store, with the family living in the floor above. Each building had its own characteristic, painted different colors, some with church windows and ornate molding. Charming.

Kimberly stood on the corner of Milwaukee Avenue and Church Street. The bookstore where they had met a week ago was just a couple of stores to the south.

Funny how we connected so fast. Unusual. I bought the book "Bridge of Desire" that day.

She stood on the sidewalk and watched the bookstore close. A summer breeze cooled down the afternoon temperature.

They always close at five o'clock. I hope he shows up soon.

She wore a beautiful silk chiffon dress of soft green and pink floral, with a high vee-neck and shawl collar, bell sleeves and a flared skirt. She carried a clutch purse.

He finally showed up in a black Cadillac convertible coup and parked next to the sidewalk, then gestured for her to hop inside. He watched as she hurried to the car. Her silk chiffon dress flowed around her body and rustled as she scooted into the passenger seat.

Removing his black fedora, he leaned over and kissed her passionately. Startled, she sucked in a breath, but did not move away. He smiled at his own conquest and shifted back into the driver seat.

"There now. That was nice."

He looked sharp in a black-pinstriped, long-length zoot suit. Olive skin. Slick hair combed back. She felt woozy as he pulled the car away from the curb.

"Where are we going?" she asked.

"We're going to the Fish Fan Club at Belmont Harbor."

Chicago. Wonder if Father will notice I'm gone. Well, I don't care. I want a good time!

She smiled back at him.

"Okay, Ricky. I'm all in."

He laughed. "Should be a ring-a-ding-ding."

He busied himself with driving until they got on a highway. That's when he noticed her perfume.

I like that.

"So, tell me about yourself," he asked.

"Nothing much to tell. Really, I'm boring. Tell me more about you," she countered. "What do you do for a living, Ricky Esposito?"

"Special tasks. Whatever Mr. Accardo wants me to do," he answered nonchalantly.

He figured, rightly, Kimberly wouldn't know the name, Tony Accardo, who worked for Al Capone while the mobster was in jail for tax evasion.

"Special tasks like what?"

"Sometimes, I'm an errand boy, delivering things, sending out messages. Other times I build small businesses and make them run. I make collections, too."

"That sounds interesting," she replied.

"It's not boring and there's moola in it."

He paused thinking about his next move.

"You know, you're cute as a bug's ear," he said glancing at her. "What do you do for a living?"

Ah, stickler subject. He doesn't know my real age.

"I'm a secretary," she lied.

He glanced at her again. *Nice dress, classy.*

"Secretary's must make some good dough. Ya know, I could get dizzy with you. You're not somebody else's moll, are you?"

"No."

"Good."

She fiddled with her clutch hand bag as if looking for something. "So, what's the Fish Fan Club?"

"Oh, you've never been there?"

"No."

"They serve different kinds of giggle juice. And the music's good. Sometimes they have a canary. It's a clip joint."

"Do you go there a lot?"

"It depends. It's not always open." He grabbed a cigarette from the pack in his pocket.

"Why?"

"Usually it's pressure from locals who don't like having hooch around." He lit his cigarette with one hand.

"Ahhh," she said. "So, who owns it?"

"Ever hear of Big Bill Thompson, Mayor of Chicago?"

"Sure."

"Well, this is his speakeasy. What a guy!"

He started laughing. "Do you know the stories about Big Bill?"

"No."

"He used to be a cowboy in Wyoming, owned some cattle. Lots of personality. He draws people to him. Just so you know, sometimes he's an egg."

Kimberly didn't notice when he checked her reaction from the corner of his eye. She was watching the passing scenery through the front window. *Okay, she's easy. Won't get upset with rough language.*

"Then he got into politics. His campaigns were hilarious! He once held a debate with two live rats."

Kimberly laughed. "How did he do that?"

"He talked a different personality with each rat, like they were in a debate. One rat was a Democrat. Kept talking about right-to-work issues, only in real vague words. Very clever! The other rat was a Socialist, who wanted a redistribution of wealth. He made his contenders look stupid."

A belly-laugh.

"Were you there?" she asked.

"Sort-a. I was making a special delivery for him while this was going on. Funny, nobody saw me. He had everyone in his palm."

She laughed again.

"After he became Mayor, he went about expanding Chicago. Post offices, freight terminals, play grounds. Folks started calling him *'Big Bill the Builder'.* He's the guy that finished building the Michigan Ave Bridge."

"Yes, I heard about that," she said. She almost made the mistake of mentioning her father.

"Then there was a period when he was going after King George V. You know, the King of England?"

She chuckled. "Why?"

"I don't know, but he said if he ever met the King, he'd punch him the face. Went so far as wanting to ban all books written by British authors."

More laughter.

"Does he know we're done with the American Revolution?"

"Yeah, he knows he's all wet. I think he does it for the laughs."

"Do you know Big Bill?" she asked.

"Yeah, I sort-a know him. My boss does some special work for him, so I've seen him around."

When they got to Belmont Harbor, Ricky parked his car and helped Kimberly out. He put his arm around her waist and directed her down the sidewalk toward a gangplank.

"Where are we going?" she asked.

"That's the gin mill," he said, gesturing to a two-story, white-painted river boat gently swaying with the water. Lights could be seen coming from inside. Jazz music wafted through the air. It was dark outside. The sound of crickets hidden in nearby bushes competed with the evening din.

"Of course," she replied.

After they were inside and shown to their table, he told her, "I heard Duke Ellington was going to be in town. Usually he plays "The Cotton Club" in New York. Lena Horne's supposed to be here, too."

Kimberly, impressed, mindfully suppressed her girlish attitude to appear sophisticated. Ricky didn't notice. He was too busy having a good time with an evening of booze, vocalists and big band music.

They were having a grand time, until the unexpected happened. On the dance floor, they bumped into Big Bill. Ricky wanted to impress Kimberly with an introduction. He tapped the big man's shoulder, indicating a conversation. Big Bill released his dance partner, looked at Ricky Esposito, then Kimberly and nodded to Ricky.

"Hey, Big Bill, I want you to meet Kimberly."

"Yes, of course," Big Bill answered carefully. "Nice to meet you."

Kimberly held her breath. "Yes, how do you do?"

Ricky was surprised at her response. Something wasn't right.

She turned to him and said, "Ricky, let's sit down."

"Okay," he replied, and then to the Mayor, "Excuse us, Big Bill." He wondered what was going on as he escorted Kimberly off the floor and to their table.

"Excuse me," she said before sitting down, and headed for the bathroom.

Big Bill saw this, excused himself from his dance partner again, and walked over to Ricky.

"How do you know her?" he asked.

"I met her at a bookstore in Libertyville. I had business there. We hit it off, bumping gums. Why?"

"Do you know who she is?"

"Yeah, Kimberly Weatherspoon."

"Of the Weatherspoon railroad magnate," Big Bill replied.

"What?"

"Yeah. That's Warren Weatherspoon's daughter. Probably sixteen years old."

"Nah, she's a secretary."

Big Bill's head tilted back as he laughed out loud. His eyes danced as if a joke had been told.

"She's not a dame. She needs a glass of milk. Now, don't blow your wig. Think about the big house."

Yikes! Big Bill knows everybody.

"Thanks, Big Bill," Ricky shook his hand and gave him a pat on his arm with his other hand. "I owe you one."

"Sure. Just get her out of here."

Ricky sat down at the table and considered how to handle this. A few minutes later Kimberly sat down next to him. She sensed what had happened.

"So why?"

"I wanted some fun and I really like you," she replied.

"Well, sweet patootie, we gotta get you out of here. Time to take you home."

The drive back was in silence.

I can't drop her off in Libertyville. It's too late. Too dark.

"How do I get you home?" he asked.

She looked at her wrist watch.

Eleven o'clock. Libertyville is closed down.

"Take me to my home. Park outside the gate and I'll walk to the house."

"In the dark?"

"I'll be okay."

He drove her where she directed, parked the car and turned off the engine. *My God, look at this place!*

The full moon shone brightly so he could see the vast Weatherspoon estate with gates wide open. Tall trees, the gardens, manicured lawns, a fountain, and the winding drive way that hinted at the grand mansion within.

"I'm sorry I lied to you." She moved closer him, her face almost touching his. She blew into his ear and kissed him on the cheek.

Damn.

He grabbed her passionately, his hands all over her as he pressed his lips to hers. She responded, urging him on. When he touched her inside thigh, she parted her knees. She gasped as he fingered her wetness. Then he placed her hand on his manhood. She pulled back for a moment, looked at him and whispered, "Yes."

They left the car and found a grassy place on the Weatherspoon property where trees and bushes provided privacy. Less urgent now, they explored each other. Soft touches, kisses. Minds melded together. They discarded their clothes slowly. She laid back on the grass and parted her knees for him to mount her. He bent over her on his knees. She looked down and saw his manhood erect. Then she looked into his eyes and welcomed him on top of her. She gasped when he entered her. The thrilling sensation when he thrust into her. Their blood had risen into an urgency that became blissful when they climaxed together. They both collapsed, hearts pounding. Restoring their breath, they canoodled in exhaustion, enjoying the moment.

Then, wakened back into the reality of what had happened, it became awkward between them. They dressed quickly in silence.

She asked, "Will you call me?"

"Sure." He finished buttoning his shirt. "Ya know, we should've brought a fire extinguisher with us."

"What?" She smiled.

"Yeah, a chaperone."

They laughed, and then he kissed her one last time.

His parting words, delivered with a casual hand wave, "Abyssinia," as he headed back to his car.

She turned away, headed for the family mansion.

He thought, *Oh My God, what have I done?*

She thought, *What a night!*

Once in bed, she slept deeply, glowing in warm satisfaction.

I really like this guy. He'll call me soon.

CHAPTER THIRTY
Contention
1933

This was a rare thing. Mr. Warren Weatherspoon opening up, showing his soft side, his fears. Mrs. Marguerite Lynn Bowles waited patiently, listening.

They were in the dining room of the Weatherspoon mansion. Kimberly was out for the evening, so they had the mansion to themselves – well, except for William. The butler knew when to appear and assist. And he knew when to disappear.

They liked it dark in that room. They sat at the far end of the large dining table. The black and white tiled floor of the grand mansion entrance was visible through the dining room archway. Silver candle holders, with stubby candles burnt down low, sent a dancing light against the walls and heavy brocade curtains. Neatly pressed table linen seemed to glow. William had cleared their dishes away. Dinner had been delicious. Dessert turned away, preferring to nurse the excellent Beaujolais.

He spoke slowly.

"I don't know what to do with her. She's nineteen, but dresses and acts like she's thirty. Head strong."

He sipped his wine, enjoying the robust bouquet. Dry. He rolled the libation over his tongue.

He whispered, "She has had many lovers, I think."

Marguerite waited, mesmerized by the energy of this moment.

"I was afraid something like this would happen. I don't know how to raise a little girl. That was the main reason I sent her to Roache. It was the best I could do."

He raised his eyes at her as if explaining. "Roache is a good school."

Marguerite reached for the bottle. The large diamond on her left had caught the candlelight, refracting light around them.

"I'll pour," he said, as he reached for her glass. He refreshed his own drink as well and sat back against his chair holding his glass with both hands.

"A couple years ago, Big Bill told me he had seen her at the Fish Fan Club. He was a gentleman about it. Discreet. My God, she was only sixteen! She was with somebody named Esposito." His voice cracked with pain. "My God, an Italian!" He raised his right hand up with fingertips together, pointing upward in a small circle.

She suppressed a smile.

He reached for a pipe from the pipe rack William had thoughtfully placed on the table, along with his favorite evening tobacco.

"Mind if I smoke?"

Marguerite shook her head.

"Do you know she was expelled from Roache Boarding School?"

The lady didn't respond.

"We had an argument about it. I told her I had looked forward to her debutant moment. She laughed at me." He loaded the pipe bowl with tobacco, struck a match and sucked until the tobacco ignited. Smoke poured from his mouth when he spoke again. "She said she wasn't a child."

Marguerite saw the pain reflected in his eyes and mouth, his drooping shoulders and the way he held his pipe.

"She keeps saying that. Even when she was small. I've never understood it…what she was saying. Do you?" His eyes looked to Marguerite, his expression desperate, pleading.

"No."

He sucked on his pipe.

"How many girls get expelled from Roache Boarding School?" he asked.

"One," she replied.

"Exactly. Something to do with the Math and Science teacher. A man. Miss Oberson was too embarrassed. Kept muttering, but was never clear."

A pause, then leaning toward Marguerite, his voice low, as if telling a secret. "I've never understood *that* woman."

Marguerite smiled knowingly.

Another pause. "Now that I think about it, I was too afraid to ask anything more." He took a few deep gulps from his wine glass and refilled it to the brim. "That child who died. I think her name was Dorothy. I can't remember if Kimberly was ten or eleven. Anyway, I've always wondered about that night. Something about it bothers me, but I can't put my finger on it. Later, when they found the killer, I just assumed the issue was over. You know, that the tragedy was done. Time to move on in life. Do you think I've made a mistake?"

"I honestly don't know," she said.

"Damn, I thought you women knew everything," he joked, then became serious again. "I'm sorry that things turned out the way they did. What do you think of her?"

She hesitated, knowing this was a moment for raw honesty.

He saw her fumbling and quickly added, "I'm sorry to ask you. I promise I won't hold it against you if you tell me the truth."

She sighed. "Well, Warren, she's an adult in her own mind. Frankly, she's not fully developed. You see, a little girl sees everything in relation to herself. As the child matures, she begins to see others outside of herself and reaches out to them. This is how things like compassion are developed. I don't think Kimberly does that. Whatever Kimberly does, it's about her."

"It's *all* about her, isn't it?" he asked.

"Yes. You have well provided for her. Maybe too well. She has not had many challenges or hardships, so she never had to learn and adjust to things."

Warren broke eye contact with Marguerite and considered his pipe as if seeing it for the first time. She watched him as the smoke trailed from his mouth. Both of them absorbed in their thoughts.

Marguerite broke the silence. "Now that you've mentioned Dorothy, what if Kimberly saw something that night, and didn't tell anyone?"

"Okay, what does it matter now?"

"Think about it. She's only ten or eleven years old. She hasn't had the time to get a proper view of life. She see's something she didn't expect. Let's say it's something shocking. She holds it inside herself. Now, and I'm speculating, it haunts her like a ghost. Something like that could affect the way she see's things, interprets things. If it's really bad, it might have stunted her development."

"How psychological of you."

She winced.

"I'm sorry," he said right away. "Here I promised to hear the truth. Please, forgive me."

"Forgiven."

"Really?" He looked contrite.

Marguerite laughed out loud. Here was this big, broad shouldered man, strong, intelligent, wealthy, influential, highly respected and feared. His contrite face did not fit her view of him.

He put his pipe on a plate. "Well, she did tell me."

"Really? When did she tell you? What *did* happen?"

"She saw the man toss the child over the balcony railing."

"Oh my God! When did she tell you? What did you tell her?"

"She told me a few weeks after it had occurred. I told her it was water under the bridge. He's in jail. Nothing can change what had happened."

"Yes, but Warren, she didn't tell the people that she should have told at the time. ***That's*** what's probably bothering her. That's what's bothering you, too."

He took more gulps of wine.

"It's in the past."

She shook her head. "No, Warren. It's in the present."

"So, what do you suggest?"

"Convince her to contact Dorothy's family and tell them what she saw. This will help release her from that experience. You too, Warren. This will help you both."

"Marguerite, you know me. Apologizing is not my bailiwick."

"You apologized to me a few minutes ago."

"Yes, I did. You're different. But to other people, I have a public image to maintain."

Oh, Warren. You're trapped in your own mind, too.

He held his hand out to her. "Shall we call it a night, Marguerite?"

She knew this was his way of asking her to stay the night with him. She considered the possibility.

He's strong, intelligent and flamboyant. Pity, he's not a good lover.

She sighed. "Yes. I'm tired, too."

They left the dining room, arms around each other and ascended the stairs, headed for his bedroom.

CHAPTER THIRTY-ONE
Prison
1935

"So, it's been ten years." Judge Weston of Chicago City gazed at the three men sitting before him.

The Judge's office was huge, due to the need to accommodate meetings for ten people. The meeting table was set at the far end of his office next to windows. Fall leaves could be seen behind the open blinds. At the opposite end of this area was the Judge's private desk, also large. A self-indulgent leather chair sat behind the desk. Perpendicular to his desk were filled bookcases that lined the walls. The arrangement designated a private work area.

Warden Joseph Ragen from Joliet Prison responded. "Correct, Your Honor, which is why I don't see the need to transfer Mr. Nacht to Joliet."

Dr. Reed had hoped to minimize contention. He chose his words carefully.

"We've exhausted possibilities to help Mr. Nacht. He's a dangerous criminal. He belongs in a prison. If you recall our discussion, we agreed to discuss a possible move to prison."

"I don't know that," Ragen countered.

Judge Weston looked at him, eyes questioning. "I have meeting minutes. Minutes that were taken ten years ago. Do you want me to read them?" The Judge gestured to a folder set on the table top before him.

"No." Ragen shrugged uncomfortably. "Look, we use isolation as a temporary solution to manage prisoner behavior. I'll have to make a process change to address this unique situation. This is difficult since I have been battling an existing infrastructure to reform this prison. Joliet has been fraught with past riots, escapes and murders. I'm trying to clean that up."

The Judge was annoyed, "I appreciate your difficulty, but I'm sure you can make the necessary changes."

Warden Ragen coughed into a handkerchief produced from his coat pocket, his irritation clear.

"I was not the Warden when this agreement was made."

"Gentlemen, Dr. Reed has carried this burden for a while now. To your point," the Judge said indicating to Dr. Reed, "I looked at the statistics you have provided regarding hospital patient demographics."

The Judge looked at the Warden again. "There is a period where population growth at the hospital was almost exponential. Do you want to see the evidence?"

The Warden shook his head. "Alright, Judge Weston. I'll accept the prisoner."

The Judge nodded. "I think that's the right decision. Gentlemen, our meeting is concluded."

A week later, Police Chief Sonne sat at the desk of his private office talking to a new recruit, Denny Lewinsky. Nineteen-year-old Denny had a husky build typical of a blond, blue-eyed Swiss. This was the main reason Chief Sonne had hired him. The man's strength had been honed from farm work and boyhood shenanigans with his three brothers.

"We'll be transporting a criminal psychopath from Elgin State Mental Hospital to Joliet Prison the day after tomorrow. We'll use a paddy wagon lent to us from Chicago. I want you to sit in the back with the prisoner."

Denny knew the Libertyville Police Force was too small to warrant their own Police Paddy Wagon.

Chief Sonne continued, "He will be handcuffed and leg-cuffed. Be aware of the man's limited stride. And be careful. Mr. Riley Nacht can be likeable. Don't be drawn into him."

Denny nodded.

"If there is a problem, bang on the inside of the paddy wagon near the driver side. I'll drive the vehicle. Another officer will be traveling with us. I'm placing him next to me. Both of us will hear you.

You will not be armed. I'm counting on you to handle the situation should Mr. Nacht become a difficulty. But don't worry. I expect Mr. Nacht to be accommodating. As a prisoner, he does not have a rambunctious history. Are there any questions?"

"Why is he so dangerous? What did he do?"

"A psychopath can be triggered by the slightest provocation. That's why you need to be careful. If he is provoked, you may not understand why. There'll be no clue, no warning."

"But what did he do?" he asked again.

"He killed three little girls. The details of what he did to them are gruesome."

Denny gasped.

"Do you think you can handle this?"

Denny nodded. "Yes, Sir."

"Okay then. The day after tomorrow we'll meet here at nine in the morning sharp."

* * *

The day of the transport turned out to be a nightmare of awful weather. The temperature suddenly dropped to near freezing. Heavy, dark gray, cumulous clouds produced relentless rain. Thirty-mile-an-hour wind gusts ripped through the traveler's coats. They rushed Riley out of "*The Hold*" and into the paddy wagon parked a few yards away. His rain coat buttoned in front, the coat-arms flapping in the wind, his hands shackled together. His leg shackles hindered the prisoner's movements and those keeping up with him. He was left chilled to the bone, soaked, unable to adjust the rain coat for better protection.

The trip took an hour and half.

Denny sat in the back of the paddy wagon with Riley. There was no heat in the rear portion of the car. Denny watched him shiver. Riley watched Denny watching him.

The men did not speak. They felt twists and turns, acceleration and deceleration as Chief Sonne drove the paddy wagon. Once, at a stop light on Archer Avenue, Denny and Riley heard the squeal of children coming from somewhere outside. Denny thought he saw Riley change for a moment. A slight smile. A crazy-eyed look. But it was fleeting.

At the same time, Chief Sonne saw a woman at the cross roads driving a two-toned Wolsey Wasp automobile through the green light. The driver was Kimberly Weatherspoon, wearing a black hat with fish netting and black gloves. He watched her turn a corner.

That's the new 1935 Wolsey salon car. Wow!

The light changed and he drove on.

The rain had stopped by the time they reached the prison.

Chief Sonne had never before been to Joliet Prison and was impressed with its foreboding appearance and size. The main building was four stories high with two-storied wings on either side. It looked like a medieval castle with towers strategically positioned for outside perimeter observation. Built in the 1850's this stone institution could hold up to twelve-hundred men.

He wondered about its' eighty-five-year-old architecture, imagining a torture chamber hidden somewhere within. He wasn't too far off. A chamber had been devised underground for prisoners sentenced to death.

While Chief Sonne made his way to the Warden's office, Denny and a prison guard escorted Riley from the paddy wagon to his new home inside Joliet Prison. Having entered the lobby of the main building, majestic and four stories high, they looked up and saw prison guards walking the perimeter of each floor, armed with rifles, looking down at them.

"Can we take off his coat here?" Denny asked the prison guard.

"Yes. You can hang it up over there," he gestured to a free-standing coat rack near the entrance's double doors.

Denny unbuttoned Riley's coat, not looking at him, and hung it up on the rack.

They headed forward until they found a stairway that took them to the second floor, toward the left wing. They passed through an iron gate, slid open by a prison guard who expected them. The guard snickered under his breath when he saw Denny jump after he banged the iron gate shut behind the three men.

They made their way through the isolation wing and found Riley's cell. It was small, six feet by twelve feet. The iron door was thick, with an open slot where a tray of food could pass, or a prisoner's hands could pass through for handcuffing. The cell had a cot, a toilet and a sink. There was no window.

Riley kept his demeanor in check even though he wanted to scream. These accommodations were severe.

The prison guard spoke. "We'll take your leg-shackles off here. Then I want you to enter your cell. After I lock the door, I want you to put your hands through the slot so that I can un-handcuff you."

Riley did as he was told as Denny watched.

After he was put away, the guard handed Denny the arm and leg shackles.

"I believe these are yours," he joked, as if an English gentleman.

"Thank you."

As they retraced their steps to the entrance, Denny asked, "How long have you been working here?"

"Almost five years."

"What's it like working here?"

"It's boring most of the time. Sometimes there are difficulties; riots, murders. The Warden is trying to fix that by stricter procedures. It's a job."

"Who is the most notorious criminal here?"

"We used to have Leopold and Loeb here. They killed a fourteen-year-old boy to prove they could commit the perfect murder."

"Yeah. I remember reading about that in the news. Golly, that was a long time ago. Weren't they students at Chicago University? Thought they were too hoity-toity?"

"Uh-huh. Eleven years ago."

"What happened to them?"

"They were transferred to Statesville Penitentiary."

"Huh. What other prisoners are here?"

"Mostly first-time offenders."

"Okay."

When the men had reached the entrance, they shook hands and said goodbye.

"Don't forget the rain coat."

"Oh yeah, thanks."

Denny made his way to the paddy wagon where the other Libertyville officer was waiting. Moments later, Chief Sonne joined them. Together the officers dropped the paddy wagon off at Police Headquarters in Chicago and made their way home by train. They chatted casually, relieved the transfer had been seamlessly executed.

* * *

Six years passed. A written appeal was made by Warden Joseph Ragen to Judge Weston and Dr. Nigel Reed.

> *Dear Sirs,*
>
> *Our ability to isolate Mr. Riley Nacht has been destroyed by a riot in that wing of the prison. As a result, Mr. Nacht has been living amongst the prison community for three months.*
>
> *During this time, Mr. Nacht has found ways to commit abnormal and egregious acts upon a subculture of adolescent homosexuals within our prison community. These are young men who look like prepubescent boys but have strong effeminate traits like little girls.*

Mr. Riley's conquests are escalating. Our prison death toll is rising. He shows no concern regarding consequences for these acts. Instead, he has become more driven to indulge in his pathological behavior.

His removal from Joliet Prison is urgent.

Know I am devoted to reform this "prison of paradise for criminals" to that of a place of meaningful reformation for those people unhindered by psychopathological challenges. I appeal to your sense-of-sense. Mr. Nacht must be returned to Elgin State Mental Hospital as soon as possible. It is my understanding his behavior was held in check while living there.

Your response to my urgent appeal is greatly appreciated by me.

Sincerely,

Warden Joseph Ragen.

CHAPTER THIRTY-TWO
Viking Trouble
1937

His eye caught the purity of her angelic, white skin and her white blond hair. What she was doing in "Andersonville" added to her mysterious façade. After all, he knew **all** his Swedish and Norwegian neighbors, mostly masons and bricklayers. Tall, muscular men, heavy-weights, with blond hair and blue eyes.

What is she doing here?

Here was the *N.N. Club*. The initials stood for "No Name". It was a speakeasy, down in the basement of a small grocery store. Living quarters were on the top floor of this two-story row home/business building. The proprietor's name was Simon Lundberg, a creative business man, who knew how to turn a dollar.

It happened innocently enough. Coffee served in the store was sometimes fortified by hard liquor. Eventually, Simon saw his coffee sales surpassed his food sales, and so the in-the-basement-speakeasy was founded. The only access via the alleyway in back. The heavy door had a slide window used for password exchange.

What is she doing here?

Over time, the *N.N. Club* became a multi-service operation. Recovering from the 1929 Depression, the laborers lost their trust in the local banking system. So, on payday Friday's, Simon would sit in his closet/office supplied with cash, under the stairs leading from the grocery store landing to the basement below. He reinforced the walls of this tiny space with steel. The door, also reinforced, had a bullet-proof window.

There was a slot in the stairway used to pass a signed paycheck and return cash. Most check-cashing establishments charged a small fee, but not Simon. He knew the money would come back to him from his illegal prohibition endeavors. On payday Friday's Simon offered a free buffet, knowing the food needed a compliment of special libations he was happy to supply.

What is she doing here?

The mahogany bar was long enough to span nearly the entire length of the building. A Victrola was placed near one end of the bar. There was a pool table nearby and scattered wooden tables and chairs. Men and women milled about. Some played pool, others cards.

Kimberly, wearing casual tan slacks and a white blouse with short sleeves, sat on a barstool with a drink – alone.

Light from the sconces on the walls bounced off the heavy red enamel paint. The wall behind the bar, mirrored. The floor tiled in a white-and-blue Delft pattern. There was an oblong stain-glass light hanging over the pool table. Decorated generally in art deco, there was an assortment of Viking paraphernalia scattered throughout, mostly etchings of Viking war ships, plus a Viking sword and helmet. The room had a comfortable feel.

Vernon pocketed the cash Simon gave him as he walked to the bar.

"Hello, I don't think we've met. My name is Vernon Lindstrom." He reached out his hand to Kimberly.

"How do you do? I'm Kimberly Weatherspoon."

"Mind if I join you?"

"Not at all."

He detected alcohol. "You're an attractive lady to be sitting all alone."

"Thank you. Sometimes I like to go where I please. Spur of the moment."

"Ah, you're emancipated, then..." He flashed his perfect white teeth in a smile.

"Completely." She tilted her head coyly.

He was dressed in a white shirt, open collar and gray pants, a fedora in his hands. He took a seat next to her and placed his hat on the bar. "So, how did you know of this place?"

"A friend told me about it. Blond haired, blue-eyed Nordic folk. I tend to like blonds, don't you?"

He laughed as he observed at her short blond hair parted to one side. Wavy. "And the password?"

She slumped over her drink with elbows on the bar. "Ah, the lady in the grocery store above."

"Of course. That's Simon's wife. He's the owner. What are you drinking?"

"I think the bartender said it's a Glogg. Vodka, spices, port wine. It's very good." She was woozy.

"I'll order one, too."

When he placed his order, the bartender gave a knowing nod.

"So, tell me about yourself, Kimberly."

She sat straight on her bar stool, swaying slightly.

"There's not too much to tell. I'm boring, really. How about you?"

He quickly took a glance at her left hand.

No wedding rings. Good.

"I work for U.S. Steel, factory scheduling manager."

"That's very important work, isn't it?"

"Yes, it is."

"Wasn't there a union strike recently?" she asked.

"Not at U.S. Steel. That was Republic Steel Company."

"Something about the union? I really don't know. I just heard about it."

He took a drink. "It's about worker's rights. Against low wages and long hours. Safety, too. The need for the company to be more responsible to their employees. U.S. Steel does that already. They have Employment Representation Plans. ERP."

"People died in that strike, didn't they?"

"Yep, sorry to say. The police killed ten people. Some of the folks here have friends who died there."

He gestured his head to the customers behind them.

"What happened after that?"

"The company hired a lawyer to negotiate with a spokesman. Yeah, the company holds all the cards. The only way to make them listen was to strike."

"Do you think that will happen at U.S. Steel?"

"Nah. The EPA will satisfy them. Why do you ask?"

"Oh, I just know someone who is in the business."

He thought a moment. *Weatherspoon, huh? A Weatherspoon wouldn't be in a place like this. Just coincidence.*

"You're an interesting dame, Kimberly. Let me buy you another drink. I'll have another, too."

When he placed his order, the bartender, wearing an apron over his white shirt and bow tie, gave him a wink and a nod.

Got it. Give her more vodka.

After the drinks were served, Vernon asked the bartender, "Buddy, put some music on, please." He turned to Kimberly. "So, really, tell me about yourself."

"There's nothing to tell. I live with my father. My mother died when I was born."

"Sorry to hear that. Got any brothers or sisters?"

She shook her head.

"I've got a sister and two brothers," he said.

"How nice for you."

"Yeah. I live alone now. Got my own place." He took her arm. "Let's dance."

He led her to an improvised dance area and started a slow dance, holding her closely. She leaned into him for support. He placed his cheek next to hers, slipped one hand down her back and pressed her against him. She felt his manliness. She didn't move away.

"Why did you come here?" he whispered into her ear.

"I wanted to get away; just stumbled on this place."

"Get away from what?"

"Things. My father."

"Well, sweetheart, I'll keep an eye on you. You're safe with me."

Somehow that made her feel good. His attention to her. Not so alone. His strength. His desire for her.

"My knight in shining armor?" She pulled away to look at him.

"Viking warrior," he corrected and pulled her back into him, cheek-to-cheek.

Something caught the corner of his eye. He took his eyes off her for a moment and saw a man he hadn't seen before. Odd, out of place. Nice black suit, but the man looked shifty. He took a seat at the far end of the bar and leaned against the wall.

Kimberly whispered into his ear. "I'm glad you're with me."

"Me, too."

Commotion. Everyone turned toward the club entryway as they heard the door slam open with a bang. A man in a dark gray suit forced his way into the speakeasy. His fedora, tilted forward, hid his face. He was holding a shot gun. The bartender stopped the music. The man in black revealed his gun.

"Everybody stay where you are." The threat made evident by the way the man in black pointed his weapon in a sweeping gesture. Using his head, he motioned the bartender to move to the other end of the bar.

Simon pulled a wire, a device he concocted to alert his wife upstairs of trouble. She alerted a policeman – on Simon's payroll.

The man in gray walked inside a few steps and stopped in front of Simon's three-inch-thick steel door. "Simon! Open the door!"

Simon kept the man busy, talking. "There's no money here. Go away!" A second later. "Okay, okay. Just a moment. I feel faint!" A second after that. "The light went out. I can't see anything. Hold on!"

Siren's heard. The robbers exchanged worried glances. Simon opened the steel door.

"Here. That's all there is." He showed the man in gray a wad of money, shoved the bills into a cloth money bag and handed it him. The man in gray grabbed the bag. Both men bolted out the door.

Like a wave, relief swept over the room.

Simon went to the bar. "Whiskey."

The bartender poured him a shot. "How much did they get?"

"About nine hundred dollars."

The bartender whistled. *Too much money!*

Simon's customers headed out the door, wanting to avoid the police. Vernon grabbed Kimberly's arm. "Let's go!"

Kimberly pulled back. "My purse!" She lost her balance and fell to the floor, backwards, her body sprawled out.

"Ouch!" She struggled to her knees.

Vernon heard the police barking orders. He bolted out the door as fast as he could, leaving Kimberly behind.

* * *

A few hours later, Warren received a call from the police.

Drunk in a low-class speakeasy. Arrested by the police. Put in jail. Oh My God!

When he hung up the phone, he reflected on the brief conversation.

The police were respectful, but had a mirthful undertone at Weatherspoon impropriety. The message was not missed: Not so hoity-to-ity, after all!

Mortified, he called his lawyer, Mr. Harold Tresling, and explained the situation.

The lawyer reassured him. "I'll arrange bond. Can you pick her up at the jail house in a couple of hours?"

"Of course. I'll send my butler."

Tresling felt badly for him. "Mr. Weatherspoon, this situation is not too bad. Money can make this go away."

"Thank you, Mr. Tresling. I appreciate your assistance."

Warren hung up the receiver.

Money can't buy self-respect.

* * *

Kimberly took the typical chair she used in Warren's office. Her father was pacing the floor behind his desk. His shirt sleeves rolled up despite his expensive suit pants and belt. She was not used to his casual appearance, nor his anger.

"You're up shits creek, young lady!"

She stayed silent, defiant, watching a wrath she had never seen before. He puffed on a cigar with intensity. She hated the stench.

"You're twenty-two years old! What the **hell** am I supposed to do with you?"

"What am I **supposed** to do?" she asked.

The question surprised him. He yanked the cigar from his mouth, placed his knuckles on his desk top and leaned forward, glaring at her like an alpha gorilla. His face blustering red.

"What?"

"What am I supposed to do, Father?"

"I expect you to behave like a god-damned lady!"

"After I behave like a god-damned lady, what am I supposed to do?"

"You're supposed to find a decent man. Get married. Have children. Be a wife and a mother!"

"Who's going to marry me, Father? There aren't that many prospects for me." She waited for this moment of gut truth, then took a breath. "Father, I have too much. No man can meet the scale that has been set for me. It's too high."

"Humph," he growled, and sat down heavily.

She has a point.

He snuffed out the cigar in a glass ashtray and used a softer tone. "So, you're just going to gallivant?"

"Why not? Things have changed, Father. Women hold jobs. Women drive cars. Women vote."

"What happened to gardening clubs?" he asked. "Reading circles? Sewing? Taking up a musical instrument. That's what real women do!"

Kimberly smirked. "I'm not one of those women. I'm more like you."

"You can't be like me."

"I can be a female version of you."

He interlocked his fingers together, placed his elbows on the arms of his padded chair.

I need to calm down.

Warren sighed, then asked, "Do you ever want to get married, Kimberly?"

"Yes, to the right man."

"I'll make a deal with you. You modify your behavior. Consider social consequences. Then you can continue to live here."

An ultimatum. Unexpected. Her face turned red. Too afraid to lash back at him.

She rose from her chair slowly her eyes engaged his. She turned and made her way to the door. Then turned again and re-engaged his eyes. It was the way she walked. Regal. Statuesque. A demonstration of her femininity. And then, her look... intense.

"Yes, Father."

She opened the door and slipped away.

Alone in his office, Warren pondered what had just happened.

*I'll be damned. She **is** just like me. Her power is just different.*

CHAPTER THIRTY-THREE
Gambling
1938

Kimberly carefully thought about her conversation with Warren. His ultimatum.

I like the freedom to do what I want when I want. My constraints are what Father expects from me – discretion. Guess I need to be more careful.

She was sitting in her room at her dressing table, looking at herself in the three-way mirror. She turned her head left to see her profile better and smiled with satisfaction.

The robbery, scary... maybe I should carry a gun... just in case. Especially if I'm going alone somewhere. Need to choose better places. No more places like the 'No Name Club'.

Then she turned her head right, examining herself in the mirror from this angle.

Okay, that's easy. I can keep on doing as I wish and keep Father happy, too. He's right, after all. I could do better.

* * *

The ladies' bathroom was located at the far end of the casino. Kimberly's hips swayed as she sashayed past the roulette table and black-jack games, certain she caught admiring eyes. The fabric of her short-sleeved, empire-waist dress draped her figure beautifully. She wore long gloves and pearls. Elegant.

I love it when men watch me.

The former Clarice Porter, now Accardo, decided to follow her.

She's old money. Privilege.

Clarice was familiar with people like Kimberly, having watched folks like her when she worked as a chorus girl. Now, married to Tony Accardo, she sometimes came to this casino.

Kimberly, at the mirror, refreshed her lipstick when Clarice entered.

"I love your dress."

"Thank you. I love your broach."

Clarice's diamond broach was pinned to a brocade bolero jacket worn over her black dress.

"My husband gave this to me for my birthday. I'm Clarice Accardo." She extended her hand to Kimberly.

Accardo. I know that name. Could she be associated with Ricky's boss?"

"I'm Kimberly Weatherspoon."

Weatherspoon. The railroad magnate?

"How do you do?"

"Fine, thank you. Would you happen to know if Ricky Esposito is here?"

Clarice was careful to respond. Her husband was a capo (mafia cap-tain) who managed Capone's gambling spots, while he served time in jail for tax evasion.

"Why do you ask?"

"We were close once. It's been a while since I've seen him."

Clarice's intuition caught the nuance of Kimberly's use of "close".

"No, I haven't seen him," Clarice lied. "Did you come here alone?"

"Yes, is that alright?"

"I suppose so…" Her voice revealed strain.

Don't like women coming alone. This isn't a brothel. We have standards.

"Are you sitting anywhere?"

"No, I just walked in."

"Why don't you join my husband and I for a drink?"

"Thank you. I'd like that."

Clarice escorted Kimberly to a table in a corner on the same side as the club's entrance. A man was sitting there with his fedora on the table, nursing a drink, watching the activity in the club. When he saw the ladies approach, he stood up from his chair. His tailored suit was expensive.

"Tony, I want to introduce you to Miss Kimberly Weatherspoon."

Tony, extended his hand. "How do you do, Miss Weatherspoon?"

Clarice continued. "This is my husband, Tony Accardo." She addressed her husband, "I invited Miss Weatherspoon to join us for a drink. Why don't you sit here?" She motioned to Kimberly.

"Please, call me Kimberly."

"And call me Clarice."

Tony, sat down and caught the eye of a waiter.

"Ladies, what's your poison?"

Clarice offered, "How about a daiquiri?"

Kimberly nodded. "Yes. Thank you."

Tony asked, "Kimberly, are you related to Warren Weatherspoon?" This was not a time to lie. "I'm his daughter."

"She was asking about Ricky Esposito," Clarice told her husband.

Tony vaguely recalled Ricky's story about Kimberly and Big Bill.

That was a long time ago. Ricky's moved on to another dame.

"I don't see him very often anymore."

"Oh..." She was disappointed. "I thought he was nice. That's all."

"Cigarette anyone?" Clarice was holding a package of Lucky Strikes. The ladies lit up.

"Do you gamble?" Tony asked.

"Not very often." She poised her head when she exhaled, lifting her nose. Kimberly didn't like this brand of tobacco, she liked the opportunity to pose, to move her body in interesting ways to capture male attention.

"Well, we have roulette, blackjack, slot machines and bingo."

As the drinks were served, Tony pointed out the different tables, explaining the games. Kimberly noticed he didn't talk about poker. All the poker tables had men – no women allowed. Most of the bingo players were women.

They chatted easily while they watched different tables from their vantage point. Tony had switched to plain water, wanting to keep his head clear.

Kimberly began to relax after her third drink. She perused the room and she spied a woman wearing a draped stole of mink pelts over her green suit. She was holding a white toy poodle, beautifully groomed.

"Who's that?" she asked Tony, pointing out the lady with her chin.

"Mrs. Cook. Her husband died two years ago. She thinks the dog is a reincarnation of him."

Kimberly belly-laughed while watching the woman throw her dice on the table. People yelled out, applauding her success. The lady put her dog down on the floor and piled her chips in front of her.

Occasional whoopla's clamored through the room from the roulette tables. Ballyhoo commotion. The warmth of the liquor removed prudent judgement.

"I think I'll try roulette," she said.

Tony encouraged her. "I can help you purchase the chips." His plan was to loan her the money, knowing Weatherspoon honor would pay the debt.

Warren Weatherspoon can't afford public embarrassment. Not with railroad money and unhappy labor clamoring at his heals.

Tony arranged for chips as Clarice followed Kimberly to the gaming table.

His back was to her, so she didn't notice him until she moved to the side of the roulette table. Handsome. Raven hair and midnight eyes. Dashing. Incredibly sexy. He moved deliberately, captivating her. She felt tingly. Aroused.

How does he do that to me?

She tilted her head suggestively and fluttered her eyes, peering at him through exhaled smoke.

Edwin Mullusio noticed her.

Clarice almost laughed out loud as she watched their dance around the roulette table, like a mating ritual between two swans. A flutter here and there, necks arched. Eyes riveted at each other, as they posed provocatively. The electricity between them was painfully apparent to Tony, who saw his chances at making a nice profit go down the drain.

On the floor underneath the roulette table, the dog stood up on his hind legs, wrapped his forepaws around Mrs. Cook's leg and started to hump. Mrs. Cook bent over and took a swipe at the dog with her arm.

"Stop that, Mr. Cook!"

Eventually, Kimberly and Edwin left the players' table together, his arm around her as they headed for the bar.

Tony, who was across the room, looked at his wife with palms up, shoulders high, as if to say, *Oh well. Can't stand between love!* Clarice chuckled and winked at her husband.

It was the beginning of an intense affair.

* * *

A couple of years had passed when Tony and Clarice read about the killing of Edwin Mullusio in the newspaper. For Tony, the story brought back memories of the hit that was made on Thomas Maloy in 1935. It went down without a hitch.

A good hit is planned in advance, cleanly executed. Dumb blond. She probably gambled her father would buy her way out of it.

CHAPTER THIRTY-FOUR
Wanting
1940

Mesmerized, Eddie watched her as she exited the police car, placing her right foot on the pavement so as to reveal the curve of her leg, enhanced by the seam of her stocking and her high-heeled shoe. She leaned forward to look at Elgin State Mental Hospital, posturing deliberately.

She wore a small navy-blue hat that matched her well-tailored suit. The color of her short, platinum-blond hair and her angel-white skin made for a striking appearance. Her lips bright red.

He stared at her.

An officer exited the police car from the opposite side of the back seat, came around and extended his hand, ostensibly to help her out of the patrol car, but also to immediately handcuff her.

Stirred by her slow-motion arrogance and privilege, Eddy's arousal came up unexpectedly from deep within. He wanted her in the worst way.

They were in bed together. Everything was white. White sheets, white pillows, white skin. Her caresses excited him. When he mounted her, her eyes became wide with wonder and then fluttered. Her red lips slightly open as she gasped softly, welcoming him into her body. He started his rhythm, whispering her name. Persephone....

Eddie, suddenly jolted, shaken from his hallucination. "What the...?"

It was Lloyd, a patient of Dr. Reed's, an imbecile and an irritant. Eddie pushed him away too hard. Lloyd fell face up onto to the sidewalk, surprised he didn't hit his head against the pavement. Eddie walked away, angry.

Lloyd got up and brushed himself off. Afraid, he looked away as Eddie stormed off. He never noticed the blond goddess handcuffed by a policeman walking through the hospital entrance.

* * *

Several weeks later, Eddie visited Riley. He did that sometimes to break up his day.

Dr. Reed had forgotten Eddie's work with Mr. Riley Fisk. Eddie had hoped recognition of his efforts would open a door for him and had been disappointed when it didn't happen. Eddie, in a sullen mood felt discarded, unappreciated.

When he walked to the security guard at the lobby of "*The Hold*", he noticed a small vase of daffodils sitting on the guard's desk. Eddie gave the guard a questioning expression.

"From my wife. Thought it would brighten up the place."

Both men snickered. After signing the log, Eddie headed downstairs to Riley's cell. He found Riley immersed in a book at his table.

"The new patient's name is Kimberly."

That one sentence grabbed Riley's attention. He put his book face down on the table top, left his chair and walked to the cell bars close to Eddie.

"Oh! Give me details. What does she look like?"

Eddie whistled; the kind of sound a man makes at a pretty woman.

"White blond hair, milky skin, flawless. Svelte. She carries herself like Gretta Garbo. There's an air about her. A goddess. I could tell she comes from privilege."

"Wow."

"Yes."

Riley put his head down in a reflective pose. "There was a child I once saw that fit that description. She was at a boarding school several years ago. There was something grandiose about her."

"Sounds like her," Eddie replied. "What are the chances it could be the same person?"

Riley looked at Eddie. "Not likely but the gods are mischievous sometimes." He paused for effect. "She's Persephone."

Eddie nodded. "In the flesh."

"Soooo? Take her…"

"What?" Eddie was thrown off balance.

Riley raised his eyebrows, suggestive. "You think we live in paradise here?"

* * *

That night, before sleep, Eddie felt tingly, aroused and something else he couldn't put his finger on. It was in his subconscious, shaken by the power of it.

Do you know how you affect me? Your softness, your looks? Your feminine mystery captivates. This is how you touch me; my groin, my desire. I want to possess you; to fill you up with me. And when I see you afterwards, I will see that empty space in me has been filled by you. You will complete me.

* * *

Kimberly looked up at the window high up in the wall of her cell and saw the blue sky. She turned her head toward the floor.

I can do this. Weatherspoon's are made of backbone, strength. That's what father always told me. We persevere, endure.

The cell, dark and damp, contained a table, a chair, a free-standing closet, a chest of drawers, a bed, several books, and two lamps. The floor, carpeted with a hand-woven Indian throw rug, was intended to make her feel cozy. All these things were her private property. Warren did what he could to provide for her comfort.

Unfortunately, the toilet was down the hall. A consequence of the old building, since the basement had been retro-fitted for different needs outside its original architectural plans. Kimberly needed to be escorted when nature called.

Over time, boredom set in. Cell walls smothering her. Outside walks were suspended because of her difficult behavior.

"You are on detention," the doctor had told her, "until you can learn to curb your behavior." Kimberly snubbed her nose at him in defiance.

I should have asked him how long my detention would last. I think they have forgotten me.

She sighed as she turned her head toward a pile of fashion magazines sent by her father. Choosing one, she sat down on a chair and flipped through the pages for the hundredth time.

She again scrutinized the dresses carefully, wondering how she would look with the latest fashion of squared shoulders, reinforced with shoulder pads. She liked the length, just below the knee, a way to show more leg. The fabrics, light and fluid. She imagined the shirt swayed as the hips moved, if one walked suggestively. The belted waistline, intended to accentuate female curves, was also something she liked.

Shoulder length hair. I'm perfect for that. Flattering! New stockings! And shoes with bows – how cute! I can have them made in any color I want.

A movie advertisement, *'The Philadelphia Story'* with Cary Grant, Jimmy Stewart and Katherine Hepburn. Articles about Judy Garland and "How to Make Your Typewriter Last."

My life is passing away in these walls.

* * *

Eddie thought about her for a long time. Plotting.

How to get into her cell. First get her cell key and duplicate it. That should be easy if I do it fast. Then opportunity – a new female hospital assistant, maybe? Someone who doesn't know the ropes at her ward, someone I can manipulate. Must keep close watch of her ward keepers.

Opportunity presented itself when a hospital assistant for Kimberly's ward had a leave of absence due to a family death.

Thirty minutes. That's all it took. The temporary ward keepers eleven o'clock nighttime lunch. The narcotic delivered in her dinner wine, another Weatherspoon luxury.

When he opened her cell door, he saw the opulence; the hand-woven rug, book shelves with books, chest of drawers, closet bureau, table and chair and freestanding floor lamp. Her bed, silk sheets and cover.

Better check she's out cold.

He bent a finger back. She should have yelled. She responded with a minor stir. He was thrilled and began to explore her body.

When Kimberly woke in the morning, she wondered why she was naked. She always slept in her silk pajamas. She felt between her legs, a sticky mess and screamed with horror.

Nobody came to her aid.

CHAPTER THIRTY-FIVE
Darren
1941

**ddie swatted the right side of his neck then looked** down at the blood on his fingers.

Damn mosquitos.

Hot outside. Humid. Summer. Mosquitos love moisture. He gazed at the man-made lake, shimmering. The hospital grounds nicely manicured, the grass recently mowed and trees in full leaf. Occasional flower beds scattered about, as well as bushes. Some patients attended to these details as part of their therapy.

He was standing on a sidewalk in front of the Elgin State Mental Hospital Administration building, waiting for a new patient to be admitted. The black bus drove up the winding road, past the man-made lake and into the paved driveway designed in a circle in front of the admission office. Only one person in the bus. Not clearly understanding the predicament of this new patient, Eddie expected to see a twenty-three-year-old man dismount the bus by himself. Instead, the driver opened the bus door and motioned Eddie to come into the vehicle. He pointed out the young man sitting far in the back. A wheel from a folded-up wheel chair stuck out in a section behind the young man.

Eddie's first experience with Cerebral Palsy. A pillow was placed behind the man's head with an end sticking out on the left side to support its weight. His arms and legs were spasmodic. Spittle rolled down his chin on the left side. Thin, too, not well shaven and dark brown hair unevenly cut. His eyes had an intelligence behind the broken body, though, and they were pleading.

"Hello. Are you Darren Owens?" Eddie asked.

"Yahha."

Scheeze. He can barely talk.

With such a variety of patients in this facility, training had been provided for caretakers like Eddie to handle most situations.

Tell the patient what will happen. Then do it.

The idea is not to surprise or frighten the patient.

The bus driver had moved behind Eddie, watching the exchange. He tapped Eddie on the shoulder.

"They gave me this." An envelope handed over.

Eddie took it, opened it and read the letter.

Sunday, August 17, 1941
To Whom It May Concern,

This is Darren Owens. He is twenty-three years old and has Cerebral Palsy. He has been under the care of his mother who passed away from a heart attack yesterday. There is no one else to care for Darren. We are sending him to Elgin State Mental Hospital for his wellbeing.

Please call Mrs. Woodrow, a neighbor friend, if you have questions: Prairie 4678.

Call Dr. Stevenson for Darren's medical history: Prairie 5291.

Eddie folded the letter, replaced it in the envelope and looked at Darren before slipping the envelope inside his pant pocket.

"Okay, Darren, we are going to move your wheel chair out from behind you and outside. Then I'll come back and carry you to your wheel chair. Okay?"

"Yahha."

Eddie looked at the driver. "Does he have anything else, some clothes?"

"Oh yeah, right here." The driver pointed to a brown leather suitcase in the seat in front.

"Good. I'll get the suitcase first."

The driver interrupted, "Nah, I can take that." He reached for the suitcase and carried it out to the sidewalk. Eddie reached for the wheel-chair and carried that outside behind him.

The driver waited as Eddie re-entered the bus.

"Okay, Darren, I'm going to lift you up now." The driver peeked inside the bus, curious.

Darren's body started to flail about which made it hard for Eddie to get ahold of him. Finally, getting his arms under this squirming muscle-mass, Eddie wrestled the bundle to balance and got him out of the bus and into his chair. Darren's head continued to flail.

"Pioowoo."

"The pillow..." said the driver, and retrieved Darren's pillow, handing it to Eddie, who tucked it in placed to provide Darren with support for his head. Next, he placed Darren's foot onto the chair's footpad.

Eddie, hands on his hips, looked at Darren more closely now. Likewise, Darren took stock of the man who had been helping him. Eddie saw intelligence in Darren's eyes.

Well, I'll be damned.

Neither men noticed the face of the bus driver, a man the same age as Darren, healthy and strong. The driver's brows furrowed with concern, his freckled face displaying heartfelt sympathy for Darren's plight. And then his gaze moved to Eddie, whose body had its own deformities. He noticed the unspoken exchange between these two men; a cockfight of male ego.

Silently, the driver walked to the bus, entered it and drove away, wondering for a moment what Darren's future would hold, then counting his blessings.

CHAPTER THIRTY-SIX
How The Gods Work
1941

When Dr. Reed entered the oblong meeting room, he saw Dr. Hoshkins and Dr. Manning already seated at the cherry-stained, mahogany table with eight chairs. The table had a green double lamp at the center. The room was also used as a medical research area. There were bookcases filled with medical books on the long side of one wall. Two windows, each with a double pane, stood opposite the bookcases. They looked out on a mature pine tree and a garden of summer flowers.

Reed chose a seat at the table near the door.

"Gentlemen, we can begin once doctors Thiele and Brenner get here."

He sat down and pulled his pipe from his coat pocket to work the tobacco. The heat of the summer day had not yet presented itself.

Dr. Thiele walked into the room as Dr. Reed lit his pipe, embers glowing as he sucked in the smoke. Dr. Brenner followed seconds later.

"Hello, Gentlemen. Sorry I'm a few minutes late." He closed the door.

"You're fine. We're just beginning," replied Dr. Hoshkins.

"Okay, the agenda. There are only four cases to discuss this morning. The Kimberly Weatherspoon case will be last," said Dr. Reed.

"That's fine."

"Dr. Manning, tell us about your patient, Darren Owen."

"Sure. An extreme case of Cerebral Palsy. Twenty-three years old. He cannot speak well and needs constant supervision. His mother passed away. The authorities had him brought here since he has no kin. A little money was left when his mother died. When that runs out, the state will fund his care."

A sigh from Dr. Reed holding his pipe. *We never have enough money to handle cases like this. At least we can start him off, and then minimize his care as best we can and still take care of the patient.*

"He's a long-term resident then. High maintenance. Let's put him in '*The Hold*' where we can maximize his care. We'll rotate nursing within our staff."

"Do you think he might be a candidate for shock therapy," Dr. Thiele asked?

Dr. Manning reached for his handkerchief inside his coat pocket, took off his glasses and wiped them.

"I suggest we consider this option after the patient has a chance to settle in and we obtain empirical information of his behavior and his needs. As you know, Cerebral Palsy is a neurological disease. I'm not sure how we can heal the patient of a disease he has had since birth. Your suggestion has merit. We can certainly look into it."

"Is there any more discussion?"

Silence.

"Next on the agenda is Betty Sacks, again, Dr. Manning, your patient."

"This one is a tragic case of syphilis. The patient is twenty-five years old, married once, then abandoned. The State Court convicted her for theft and prostitution. She has no family. She requires restraint since she often becomes hysterical. We are using opium occasionally to calm her, but we know we cannot use this method as a long-term solution. We've tried cold baths, but this method is ineffectual."

"I think she could be a candidate for lobotomy," offered Dr. Hoshkins. "I can make her calm, easily manageable and happy."

"I was hoping you would say that, Doctor. Narcotics will exacerbate the problem in the long run. If agreed, let's schedule the operation as soon as possible.

Heads nodded. Dr. Reed took a pull on his pipe, exhaling a thin stream of smoke.

"The next patient is Alice Polaski, the Downs Syndrome girl. How did the sterilization go?"

Dr. Hoshkins replied, "The tubal ligation went well. The patient is recovering, but I do have an alarming event to report."

A breath.

"When I inserted the clamp into the vagina and dilated the cervix, I examined the patient to make sure she was healthy, that there would be no surprises. I found evidence of semen."

A gasp filled the room.

What?

"She's only fourteen."

"Precisely."

A fourteen-year-old girl with Downs Syndrome. How could this happen?

"Gentlemen, we have a problem on our hands." Dr. Hoshkins interlocked his fingers, placing his elbows on the table. He looked at each physician one by one.

"She must have been violated by someone in our hospital."

Shock. Silence as each doctor considered the meaning of this terrible incident. Dr. Reed broke the silence.

"An investigation is needed. Utmost discretion. This cannot come out to anyone."

"Who do you suggest? Eddie Fisk?"

"No. The investigation must be conducted by someone in this room."

A pause. Nobody wanted to volunteer for this ugly task.

"Alright, I'll do it," Dr. Reed said. "I'll come up with a strategy to handle this discreetly. Meanwhile, I want a female nurse's aide with her constantly. I do not want Alice Polaski to be alone. No male attendant at all."

Nodding heads in unison indicated agreement.

Dr. Hoshkins, "I'll make sure she does not leave the female quarters for rest of her stay. Her parents will be taking her back home at the end of the week."

The pipe smoke bellowed from Dr. Reed's mouth. "Good to know. I may ask her questions so I can figure out what had happened."

"Do we tell the parents?" Dr. Thiele asked.

Another draw from the pipe. "Absolutely not. To what end would we do that? No. This stays here in this room." He placed his pipe on the table.

Dr. Thiele clenched his lips together, his eyebrows furrowed. "I understand the need for discretion, Dr. Reed…but…respectfully, Sir, you do not come from a neutral position. I propose neutrality is needed, so the investigation will be effective."

"Do you volunteer, Dr. Thiele?"

"No."

"Do we hire an investigator? Do we tell her parents? Shall we notify the newspapers? How about a radio announcement?" Dr. Reed was pissed. His eyes bore into Dr. Thiele's eyes, who then turned away.

"She might tell her parents something happened."

Dr. Reed fiddled with his pipe for a moment, thinking.

"I said I'll talk to her, Dr. Thiele."

Silence filled the room. An unspoken agreement. Dr. Reed will ask Alice questions and figure out how to diminish her experience, if she seems upset. In reality, nothing more would be done.

"Let's continue now," Dr. Reed sighed. "Our last patient, Dr. Hoskins, is Kimberly Weatherspoon."

"Of course," Dr. Brenner said. "She has been in isolation, but has become a problem when she needs to be escorted to the bathroom. Kimberly is a very difficult patient, much more combative, hostile and physically strong. She has tantrums. Curiously, she's been telling us, for several months now, that she has been violated. I believe this is a hallucination. A man cannot get into her cell. My opinion is she's acting out hysterically."

Dr. Reed fiddled with the pipe on the table.

"Isn't that strange though? We have a fourteen-year-old girl and Miss Weatherspoon?"

"I think it's coincidence," Dr. Brenner replied. "Weatherspoon is not a reliable source. She'll do anything to get out of her circumstances."

Dr. Hoshkins suggested, "What about lobotomy?"

Dr. Brenner thought out loud, his hands clasped together with his elbows on the table. "She's a puzzle with a complicated history. A spoiled narcissist with no morals. To be honest, that's really why she's here. This fact was acted out in murder – something she thought she could get away with. Narcissists are self-absorbed, privileged. And she's rich with the Weatherspoon legacy, which reinforces her illness. Her family position makes her a danger to our hospital should anything go awry. Do you think an operation can fix all that?"

"Yes." Dr. Hoshkins replied. "In fact, when I schedule the lobotomy for Betty Sacks, I can also schedule the same operation for Kimberly Weatherspoon."

Dr. Brenner looked at Dr. Hoskins, unclenched his hands, palms exposed and relented with nod.

Dr. Reed took another long draw from his pipe.

"Wonderful. Dr. Hoshkins, give Mr. Warren Weatherspoon a call today and see if you can get his permission first. I've spoken with him before. He'll probably agree. Then, schedule the operations."

Dr. Reed emptied his pipe into the ashtray on the table.

"Are there any other issues to address before we continue with our day?"

Shaking of heads.

"Thank you, gentlemen. Have a good day."

Dr. Brenner, the last man to leave the room, closed the door.

Kimberly Weatherspoon, another name for whore.

CHAPTER THIRTY-SEVEN
Destrui
1941

Ten months had passed since her first entry into her cell. Back then she had shrugged off her predicament, expecting her father to save her. Instead, her father had made her accommodations as comfortable as possible. Unexpected.

Kimberly could hear the wind outside. She looked up at the window high up in the wall of her cell and saw gray cumulous clouds pass by. She turned away, the thoughts in her head rambling.

Must be the beginning of fall. Maybe a storm.

Her cell was too warm. Stuffy. She could not find a way to escape the suffocation.

I am so bored.

She looked up toward her window again. A plane! It suddenly disappeared from her view.

I don't need to see you. I hear you in the crevasses of my heart. A plane, engine rumbling in low tones. You own the air of freedom. The open space so welcoming. It must be glorious to ride the air with wings. I was not so blessed. But I did notice those given this blessing. Swans, snow geese, cranes and pilots. I am in awe of you. Given the ability to hop from cloud to cloud. I would give anything to be you.

* * *

Off and on, the smell of neighboring incarcerated female prisoners was overwhelming; urine, excrement and blood from the monthly cycle in a pail. Even the hospital staff would wear masks to abate the stink when they come into these cells to remove the pail's foul contents.

No way to escape this in-the-basement prison of women inmates.

Some neighbor screamed. The pitch nerve wracking, spine-tingling. Finally, too exhausted to utter another sound, the unknown female passes out. The excruciating acoustics fall into silent agony.

Kimberly cannot see the screamer's matted hair. The oily skin peppered with dirt. Her body like a skeleton, she will not eat.

* * *

Dead time passed. Kimberly lay on her bed, hands behind her head, feet crossed, staring at the ceiling, thinking. Roache Boarding School and Miss Oberson came to mind. The classes: "The Elements of Decorating – Color Schemes", "Purchasing Furniture, Bedding and Bathroom Accoutrements", "Fundamentals of Philosophy", "Developing Talent for Entertaining Well", "Art Design", "Convivial Conversation".

I remember Dorothy and the geisha doll. We WERE being groomed. I didn't realize it at the time.

She recalled the Math and Science teacher and his gray handle-bar mustache, too big for his narrow face.

Mr. Turner was his name. Tall man, lanky. He talked about the 'perfect ratio' and he showed my face in front of class as an example. Of course, I'm perfect. I remember he mentioned "bodily curves". Later the man fondled my breasts. Why didn't I push him away? Ah... because I was never taught to do that. Not lady-like.

She glanced up at the window contemplating freedom. Then her thoughts went back to that incident.

Miss Oberson's face went beat-red when I told her what had happened. I suppose it was good that I was expelled.

A knock on her cell door.

"Kimberly?"

"Yes?"

She heard the latch of her cell door being opened. The woman wore a nurse's uniform. Another woman, the cell keeper, was standing behind her.

"Hello. I'm Nurse McKinsey. How are you, Kimberly?" The nurse did not wait for an answer. "Tomorrow, you are scheduled for a treatment. You'll get showered first and you'll be given a fresh smock to wear.

"What sort of treatment?" she asked.

"Didn't your doctor tell you?"

Kimberly shook her head.

"Oh, my goodness." She gave an apologetic expression. "It's a special treatment to make you feel better. I'll ask him to come by your cell later today so you can ask him any questions you may have. Meanwhile, he wants you to take this pill. Okay?"

The nurse extended her hand holding a pill, the other a glass of water.

Kimberly did as she was told and swallowed the pill.

"Good! Tomorrow I think you'll have a good day."

The cell door closed.

She lay down on her bed again, wondering, again, about her future. Overwhelmed with sorrow, she sobbed into her pillow before she fell into a deep sleep. The doctor never came.

CHAPTER THIRTY-EIGHT

Tartarus

1941

Darren looked at his new surroundings, a small room with a bed, chest of drawers, and an adjoining lavatory. Simple, sparse but adequate, with just enough room for his wheel chair in a space between the bed and the far wall. Perpendicular to the far wall and over the head of the bed a coal-gas appliance provided bright light.

An attendant wheeled him into the room and asked, "Which is easier, this side of the bed or that?"

Darren pointed to the far wall and said, "Th-ah-t."

Using their coordinated efforts, the attendant helped Darren into the bed.

"I'll be right back," he said, taking a final glance at Darren. He noticed the too-bright light shining on Darren's face and halted for a second thinking he should adjust it. A stench filled the room, unfamiliar, and he figured it came from Darren. He did not notice the missing wire mesh that should have been anchored to the light base.

He left the room and closed the door behind him.

Darren looked up at the bright light and reached for it. His arm flailed in a seizure spurred by the sudden movement. Too close, the sleeve of his cotton shirt caught fire, engulfing him in flames. The fire raced down the connector pipe.

* * *

Dr. Reed started his day going over patient records. Disturbed with Riley's lack of progress, he reflected.

What to do with Riley. It's like a satire on Broadway. A dance with the gods.

The doctor imagined a colorful display of clown-like, Greek gods on stage, running around in organized chaos, with a soprano dressed as Athena singing a long, high-pitched note. Jarred into reality, he jumped when his desk phone rang.

"Hello."

"Dr. Reed, there's a fire in *'The Hold'*!"

"Oh my God."

"I've called the fire trucks."

"Can you get the patients out?"

"I don't know yet."

"I'm coming."

He hung up, hurried toward the door, and ran down the staircase to his secretary's desk. "Stephanie, find Eddie and tell him to get to *'The Hold'* fast."

She didn't respond, aware of his urgency, and picked up the receiver and dialed.

"It's a fire," Dr. Reed shouted back over his shoulder as he ran to the building's front door. He sprinted to his car and drove to *'The Hold'*.

Flames were observable from the building's first floor.

* * *

Down in the basement, Eddie scratched his ear as he listened to Riley. The professionalism that declared their initial relationship gone. They were friends now, sharing a common thread.

"Hades holds the secret places of the earth, caverns and caves and water, like a woman before menses. This is why Persephone became Hades wife. She's close to mother earth, especially during the spring season when she is most radiant. Her beauty tortured men living in hell after she became his wife."

Eddie laughed at the absurdity, but noticed Riley's seriousness.

"Ah! Her beauty was her weakness that Hades enjoyed personally. As a god of the underworld he used it as a strength."

Riley's demeanor changed into something half-crazy, but Eddie didn't care. The men were standing close together, facing each other, with the jail bars separating them as they both stood leaning against the common wall.

"It's analogous to the stars. The transformation between weak and strong forces. We see it everywhere. The strong becomes the weak and the weak becomes the strong. It's fluid, cyclical. Consider black holes in the universe, for instance. Even light cannot escape them."

"What?"

"Black holes. Neutron stars that have collapsed into black holes. Even gravity does not escape."

"Huh…" Eddie sighed, fascinated. *It's amazing what Riley comes up with.*

"That's what's so miraculous. Big-bang from an atom? Prior to the big-bang event is the black hole collapsing into an atom. That's what I believe, anyway. And it's surrounded by time. Time is the only thing that does not change…well…it bends…"

"Huh?"

"Yes, there is a geometric property to spacetime."

"That's too hard for me to think about," Eddie confessed.

Riley appreciated his truth. "It is hard," he said. "But it's there. It depends upon the perspective of the observer – time and place of an event."

"Isn't that true everywhere?"

"Precisely."

A pause. Eddie asked, "Cronus, the God of time. Is he in the stars?"

"He's Saturn."

"And Zeus, in the stars?"

"Jupiter."

Eddie reflected, "Cronus was a god-king before Zeus, and then Zeus became the god-king."

"That's right. Cronus did not want to be overcome by his offspring, so he killed them at birth; all except Zeus, who escaped."

"I'm starting to understand what you see. It's what you said, the cycle of weak forces and strong forces. Everything changes. Nothing stays the same. And mythology, the gods, talk about higher ideals. Endurance, for instance, in the middle of never-ending transformations. Even the changing seasons on earth, which are obvious, is something you think about differently. But you, Riley, also see it in the stars, in the universe and in the infinitely small. You see what most others cannot see. I also understand how big all this is. It's overwhelming. It's everything."

Riley became teary-eyed. His lower lip slightly trembled.

Silence – and then Eddie continued, "Nobody understands you, and so you're alone most of the time. I'm alone most of the time, too."

Then, Eddie tried something new. "Which one of the gods do you closely identify with?"

"There is no god of poverty," Riley replied. "Maybe the closest thing is primordial Tartarus."

Sudden shouts from above and within the cells of *'The Hold'* interrupted them. Eddie moved down the prison hall to inspect. He could see flames consuming a connector pipe that ran down a far wall. Soon all the cells would be engulfed in fire.

He ran to the end of the hall, opened the heavy door that separated this maximum-security dormitory and found the stairway torched, the smoke thickening. He slammed the door closed, turned around and looked at all the faces filled with questioning expressions peering at him through their cell bars. Eddie made eye contact with them all - fear. Some of the men screamed, shaking the bars. Others accepted their fate and prayed.

Eddie took a deep breath, opened the door and ran up the stairs a fast as he could. Each step taken an agony of heat, blistering pain that started to overwhelm him. He reached the first-floor landing. Two prison officers saw him, hurried to his aid and extinguished the smoldering fire on his body. Together they dragged him out of the building to a waiting ambulance.

As the medical team worked over Eddie, he looked around his environment in spite of the searing pain, his heart beating too fast. The fresh air consoling and people hurrying about him gave him calm. Then he saw her. Kimberly's blond hair, shaved to skin, was growing out. Her white skin, exquisite facial features – her body frail and thin. She was in a wheel chair, a few yards away. The nurse behind her observing the calamity of the fire, the expression contorting her face proclaimed the severity of this accident. Kimberly's expression was devoid of emotion – like a mannequin in a store window.

Eddie gasped at the swift sharp feeling in his chest. His face registered surprise. The deep intake of breath, his last. The final beat of his heart went unnoticed.

Below ground level, Riley pondered Tartarus, dark energy, a black hole said to be the initial source of cosmic light in Greek mythology. He also thought of Hephaestus, the god of fire, the only one among the gods that was ugly and deformed. Eddie.

The irony of it made him smile and gave him solace. Validated, once again. The gods were true. He accepted his fate with peace.

CHAPTER THIRTY-NINE
Roll Of The Dice
1941

Ten men died in the fire.

Eddie's elderly parents grieved terribly when they buried him at the Elgin State Mental Hospital graveyard. Dr. Reed gave a glowing soliloquy, a sincere appreciation for his work. His words made Mr. and Mrs. Fisk feel proud of their son.

Riley, too, with gravestone marked. The location gained a reputation of notoriety with claims that a soft light could be seen above his grave on moonless nights. Others reported a soft groan, sometimes male, other times female, coming from that direction. So brief. The source of the sound spurious. Passers-by questioned their own sense of reason.

The other men, with no kin, were buried in unmarked graves, unceremoniously.

Damage to the maximum-security building for men was extensive. Dr. Reed made sure the facility was in operation within a few weeks. The demand too great to delay. The old lighting system finally replaced with an electric system. New safety procedures put into place.

* * *

Soon after, Elgin State Mental Hospital became fully operational, with events typically erupting as the mentally ill struggled with escalated symptoms requiring immediate attention. However, on most days, right after dinner, there was a time slot where peace prevailed.

Their appointment had been scheduled for this period. The purpose, to discuss the post-operation progress of his patients, Kimberly Weatherspoon and Betty Sacks.

Dr. Reed finished signing the last page of a small stack of papers just as Dr. Hoshkins entered his office. Their eyes met as he put the papers in the top drawer of his desk.

"Hello, Doctor. How about a shot of whiskey?"

"Sure. Appreciate it."

Dr. Reed retrieved a flask of clear liquid and a couple of tumblers from his bookcase, then poured their drinks. "How are Miss Weatherspoon and Miss Sacks doing?"

"Miss Sacks is doing well. Her recovery is going beyond what we expected. She's amenable and happy, as if a weight has been lifted off her psyche. She remembers most things, but has forgotten a couple of simple issues with personal hygiene and dressing herself. This is not surprising. She can re-learn these things. I think she can be released in a few weeks. It depends upon how quickly she adjusts."

"Favorable results, then. Is she truly happy?"

Dr. Hoshkins smiled and nodded. "Yes, and grateful. This one, I believe, is a success."

"Do you think she can learn a trade?"

"Yes, I think she can. Seamstress, perhaps. We'll see if she likes the idea."

"Very nice," said Dr. Reed, pleased. "We'd like to see her be self-sufficient. This would be a boon to our approach to mental health. We need more successes like this."

"Agreed."

Dr. Hoshkins paused to take a gulp of the alcohol. He became nervous. "Unfortunately, Miss Weatherspoon's reaction is completely opposite. She's docile and apathetic. She will respond, if encouraged, but she rarely initiates a thought or an action of her own. Frankly, she's not the woman she once was. She's more like an adolescent without the willfulness."

Dr. Reed frowned, looking down, elbows on the desktop, fingertips touching, fingers spread apart. *There are risks with this approach.*

Dr. Hoshkins asked, "Does she need to be self-sufficient? Learn a trade?"

Dr. Reed looked at Dr. Hoskins. "No. I think Mr. Weatherspoon will accept this outcome if I explain it to him – that Kimberly is not an adult anymore, but rather more like a child. The main thing is, she will not be disruptive and difficult, which was his primary concern. He has resources to provide for her needs. Frankly doctor, her father's desire was that her behavior change into something within the expectations of society. Have we succeeded?"

Dr. Hoshkins reflected upon these words. *The expectations of society. She doesn't have to do anything.*

"Yes and thank you for putting it that way."

Dr. Reed nodded. "Everything will be fine. How about we call it a day?"

"Of course. Thank you, Dr. Reed, and have a good evening."

CHAPTER FORTY
Kimberly Returns Home
1942

Mr. Warren Weatherspoon hung up the phone receiver, pondering the conversation he had just had with Dr. Reed at Elgin State Mental Hospital. Overall, Kimberly's lobotomy had been successful, but there were residual effects that needed attention. There were things she didn't remember, which reportedly could be addressed by re-learning. Dr. Reed estimated her personality had regressed to that of a thirteen-year-old.

Warren recalled a hopeful comment. "She will be able to re-learn quickly. In fact, the nurses have already helped her with reading skills. Her personality change, however, is permanent."

He considered the future, and what future circumstances might need to be faced.

What to do next. It's clear Dr. Reed doesn't want to keep her at the asylum. Too expensive, too demanding. Can I bring her home?

Tresling, Kimberly's defense attorney. Warren flipped through his Rolodex, found the number and dialed. Tresling's secretary put him on hold briefly.

"Well, hello, Mr. Weatherspoon! How nice to hear from you." Tresling sounded genuinely pleased.

"I hope I didn't catch you at a bad time."

"No, not at all."

"It's about Kimberly. She's had an operation and her doctor thinks she should come home. He believes she has been cured, that she's not insane anymore. Can you arrange her release from the hospital?"

"Why don't you come into the office tomorrow so that we can discuss that."

"Thank you. I'll be there at one o'clock in the afternoon."

* * *

It took several months to gather convincing evidence reassuring the Judge that Kimberly had been cured and should be remanded to her father's care.

Toward that end, Dr. Reed wrote a dissertation to the Judge, pointing out diminished state funds and a rising population at the hospital, which interfered with their obligation to provide adequate care for Kimberly Weatherspoon. After a convincing testimony, the Judge relented.

* * *

The hospital staff prepared Kimberly for her exit from Elgin State Mental Hospital. Most of this was easy paper work but arranging for the removal of Kimberly's property from her cell was a complication that required the assistance of Warren's capable secretary. This final detail was scheduled for a time after Kimberly would exit the premises. Warren requested these articles be given to a charity, not wanting these items to remind Kimberly of her time at Elgin.

After signing the hospital's papers, Warren saw her for the first time. *My God, it's been two years and two months since I've seen her.*

She wore no makeup. Her blond eyebrows and white skin allowed her natural beauty to be visible. Her navy-blue dress conservative. Her exit clothes, previously purchased by Warren's close friend, Mrs.

Marguerite Lynn Bowles. Important Kimberly be properly dressed for her homecoming.

Kimberly's demeanor subdued. Waiting for instructions, not knowing what to do. Warren, kind and careful, watched her closely. The ride home, in silence.

The black Cadillac Sedan passed the gatehouse and paused. The gatekeeper, inside the small structure, pressed a button to open the white iron gates. The magnificent Weatherspoon landscape laid just beyond. When the automobile could pass through, it started up the winding pavement toward the Weatherspoon mansion.

Kimberly gazed through the car window as the car passed deep green pine trees, tall oak trees with red leaves, manicured patches of lawn, still green, and fall flower beds of orange and yellow mums. *Beautiful colors. Everything so fresh. Day light!*

The car stopped in front of the mansion. The driver got out, opened the door. and helped Kimberly from the car. Her black-gloved hands smoothed her navy-blue, mid-calf-length wool coat. Her shoulder-length blonde hair rustled in the breeze.

Mr. Warren Weatherspoon opened his own back door and made his way around the back of the car toward his daughter.

"Thank you," he said to the driver. "Will you please take her bag into the house?"

"Yes, Sir."

Kimberly breathed in the cool fall air while she looked up at her surroundings. Her eyes scanned the front of the mansion. Six columns, a long porch and heavy wooden, double, front doors with impressive brass lion-head door knockers.

I knew this place once. It gave me pleasure to be here.

She turned her eyes to Warren, who looked at her tenderly. "It's good to have you home, dear. Let's get you settled in. I have kept your room exactly the same."

He took her arm as they walked up the three stairsteps to the porch, and then to the front door.

The driver, holding a suitcase, followed from behind.

Warren opened the front door just as William walked past the spiral staircase and across the black-and-white-diamond-tiled floor of the entryway toward them.

"Welcome home, Miss Kimberly," he said.

The couple walked into the house and Kimberly paused while she looked around.

William took Kimberly's suitcase from the driver and dismissed him, then waited for Kimberly's reaction to her homecoming, as did Warren. They watched as she scanned the entryway.

Straight ahead and high up was a balcony that launched stairs, flowing down to the first floor. Beneath the staircase, a small door leading to the kitchen. To the left, a portrait of Mr. Weatherspoon holding a gold, Elgin-made pocket watch in one hand and a Bible in the other. The image of a large, black locomotive chugging along train tracks in the background. Next to the portrait, the drawing room entrance.

Is she going to remember? Warren caught himself holding his breath.

She took a couple steps toward the drawing room, not recognizing it.

"We've re-decorated the drawing room. I hope you like it."

She turned to him. "I don't remember."

"Don't worry, my dear. You've been through a lot. Some things you'll remember, and some things not. Don't concern yourself."

She pointed to the door underneath the stair case. "What is that door?"

"It goes to coat closets and a hall leading to the kitchen."

Warren turned to the butler. "Will you please take her bag to her room?"

"Of course." William left them.

Kimberly entered the drawing room. It didn't seem familiar. Warren followed. "Take off your coat. Let's walk through the house. I'll show you where we have made changes."

Obediently, she unbuttoned her coat, slipped it off, and laid it on a cloth covered padded chair.

Exiting the drawing room, they walked through the entryway, past the staircase landing, and to the left, down a hall.

Warren stopped and opened the first door. "My office hasn't changed. Do you remember it?"

She walked into the room and smelled the scent of her father's favorite pipe tobacco. She looked at the heavy mahogany desk and the pictures on the wall.

Everything in this room is big. I don't remember.

They continued down the hall to the billiard room.

"The billiard room is exactly the same."

She peeked through the door and saw mahogany paneling and pine green taffeta walls. Hovering above the mahogany billiard table was a stained-glass light fixture that matched the stained-glass windows on one side of the room. A liquor bar was at the far end, with crystal tumblers and liquor bottles on the wall behind it.

She nodded to her father. This room made her uncomfortable.

Taking a step from the doorway, she staggered, then leaned against the door-frame.

"Are you alright?" Warren reached for her, but stopped short of actually touching her.

"I'm suddenly tired."

"Of course. I'll take you to your room."

Walking back toward the entryway, they turned right and up the stairs, past the balcony, and down the hall.

"Here is your room," he said. He opened the door for her.

Wispy-feeling. Afternoon sunlight passed through ivory curtains, hung in a crisscross fashion, left muted sunshine on the carpeted floor. She looked at the single-sized bed, plump with a satin quilt. Canopy-cover similar to the curtains. There was a chest of drawers and a triple-mirrored dressing table with a skirt. To the left were two doors.

Comforted, Kimberly sighed, but did not move. Warren realized she didn't know what to do.

Stepping from her side for a moment, Warren called for William using the intercom. "Will you please find a maid to help Kimberly?"

"Yes, Sir."

A maid came running up the stairs with William immediately following, concerned.

"Please, help Kimberly get settled into bed," Warren instructed the maid.

"Yes, of course."

Then he turned to his daughter and kissed her on the cheek. "I'll see you in the morning, dear."

The two men left the room. William closed the door and headed down the stairs behind his master.

Warren considered his daughter. *Hmmm. She has changed. Definitely less exuberant, less brash. Not as superficial as she once was. Not self-centered, demanding. If this is true, I am delighted.*

The maid drew her bath water, helped her undress and pulled back the bed covers. Kimberly watched the maid pitter-patter about the room.

When did I last have a bath?

The hot water refreshed her. Relaxing.

She donned the pretty night gown the maid had laid out for her and looked at herself in the mirror. Nothing stood out as special. She slowly made her way to her bed. The scent of Lavender filled her senses. A sachet tucked inside her pillows.

Kimberly noticed a drawer in the side table. She pulled it open and discovered a small, framed photo of a smiling man in t-shirt and shorts. He had raven hair and midnight eyes. There were sweat stains on his shirt. A lake in the background. A glint of sunlight, reflected from the gold watch he wore, caught her eye.

For a second, something in her stirred, followed by an empty feeling.

She tossed the picture in a nearby trash can and lay back against the pillows for a much-needed rest.

CHAPTER FORTY-ONE
Fantum
1942

William, now fifty-nine years old, sat alone at the kitchen table sipping a cup of coffee. Too early in the morning, he appreciated a moment of quiet solitude in the Weatherspoon mansion. These were moments of reflection and planning for the day's events.

This time though, his thoughts were of Kimberly. She had come home the day before and William wanted to think about how Kimberly – the way she was now – would affect running the household.

He also needed a moment to mourn her. The young woman who had arrived from Elgin State Mental Hospital was not the same person who had left this house long ago. She was an imposter who looked like Kimberly but did not act like her.

She's gone. I can't believe what happened to her. Her body is there but her soul is gone. A light has faded away and is now extinguished.

Painfully aware that a maid could not handle Kimberly's needs, William had quickly secured the services of a nurse. She was scheduled to arrive this morning.

He enjoyed the bouquet of fresh coffee, then shuddered at the thought of brain surgery. Taking a sip, the warm liquid helped deflect the chill that had stiffened his spine.

He checked his watch. Nurse Jacobs should be arriving in an hour. He rose from the table, set his cup in the kitchen sink and headed for the servants' quarters to dress for the day.

An hour later, fully dressed, William entered the kitchen and saw the cook making breakfast. He then headed to the dining room to set the morning table. When everything was in order, he checked his Elgin-made watch.

Hmmm. Unusual. Mr. Weatherspoon is never late.

He made his way up the stairs to Warren's bedroom and knocked at the door. He couldn't make out the response, so he opened the door to peer inside.

Unprepared for the scene before him, William startled at what he saw. Mr. Weatherspoon lay in his bed, confusion evident on his face. Slimy spit had made its way down the side of his face and collected on his pillow. The man struggled to move his body. He could not speak coherently.

William rushed to him, alarmed, knowing he needed to calm Warren down. William took his hand and bent over Warren's face. "I'm here. Don't worry. I'll call the doctor immediately. I'll be right back!"

They both heard a knock at the mansion front door.

"That's a nurse, thank God. I'll be right back."

William left Warren, rushed down the stairs and opened the door.

"Thank God, you're here, Miss Jacobs. It's Mr. Weatherspoon. Something has happened. I'll show you the way."

The nurse, sensing the urgency, responded with, "Of course," and ran up the stairs behind William into Warren's room.

Stepping aside for the nurse to take over, William then saw her medical bag and noticed the cape she wore over her nurse's uniform. Her nurse's hat was pinned to her light brown hair.

She tossed her cape over a nearby chair, took a stethoscope from her bag, and then gave Warren a cursory examination.

"Possible stroke, or heart attack," she said matter-of-factly. "Call the doctor and the ambulance right away."

William snatched up the phone in Warren's bedroom and made the two calls, while Nurse Jacobs spoke to Warren. "Mr. Weatherspoon, I will make you as comfortable as possible. I know cardiopulmonary resuscitation so I can save your life if needed. Relax. Try to breathe normally. We'll get you to the hospital as quickly as possible."

Mr. Weatherspoon used his eyes to indicate he wanted William. When the butler hung up the phone, Nurse Jacob said, "He wants to tell you something."

Warren struggled to speak, finally getting out one syllable. "T-Tres…."

"Tresling?" William asked. Warren blinked hard, just once, telling the butler 'yes'.

"Of course, I'll tell him to see you."

The ambulance arrived at the Weatherspoon mansion in minutes and hastened to prepare Warren for the trip to Elgin State Mental Hospital.

"The doctor will meet you at Elgin, Mr. Weatherspoon," the emergency technician told him. "Relax. We'll do everything. You are in good hands."

Warren had never felt so helpless. The pain, the fear, the inability to speak.

Oh God, NOT Elgin State Mental Hospital!

Both William and Nurse Jacobs were there to close the mansion front door as the ambulance wound up its sirens and wailing urgency, sped away from the property.

William, shaken, looked at the nurse and said, "Thank God you were here. I can't thank you enough."

"I'm glad I was here, too," she said, nodding. Then she looked up the stairs, pointed, and asked, "Is that where Miss Kimberly Weatherspoon is?"

"Yes. I'll show you to her room."

"Before we do that," Nurse Jacobs interrupted, "is there a family member, someone that can go to the hospital, to be with Mr. Weatherspoon?"

William thought for a moment. "I'll call Mrs. Marguerite Bowles."

"Good. Show me to Kimberly's room, and then call Mrs. Bowles and tell her what has happened."

It was Nurse Jacob's tone that William found consoling; that somebody had a clear head and knew what to do in an emergency.

They made their way up the stairs. William knocked on Kimberly's door, and then entered with the nurse behind him. They heard Kimberly in the adjoining bathroom. The nurse walked in front of William and knocked on the bathroom door. "Kimberly?"

William retreated to the bedroom doorway, not wanting to witness delicate female privacy. The nurse opened the door slightly and peeked inside.

Kimberly was standing in front of the bathroom mirror. Her disheveled hair and wrinkled nightgown indicated she had recently 'roused from her bed. Turning toward the nurse, Kimberly's eyes widened when she saw the nurse's cap. Her body stiffened and she took a step away from Nurse Jacobs.

Nurse Jacobs saw the alarm reflected on Kimberly's face. She chose a nonchalant response and opened the door a bit wider.

"Hello, my name is Judy Jacobs. I've been hired by your father to assist you."

Intuition told Judy to remove her cap. She smiled at Kimberly, as if her actions were natural.

"I hope you don't mind if I get rid of this thing," she said. Then she shook her head to free her hair and it fell to her shoulders. Kimberly watched Judy and started to relax.

Eureka! A successful step. "I am sorry if you don't like my uniform. It's all I have to wear today."

"That's okay," Kimberly replied haltingly.

"How about we get you showered and dressed for the day?"

Kimberly nodded her head. "Can we go outside afterwards? Fresh air?"

"That's a great idea. It's a beautiful fall day. Let's do that after breakfast."

William heard the conversation, stepped out of the doorway into the hallway, and closed the door with a sigh of relief. He dabbed perspiration from his forehead with his handkerchief, as he made his way down the stairs. Then he tucked it away in his breast pocket.

Now to call Mrs. Bowles.

* * *

Marguerite, sitting in a comfortable chair in her bedroom, hung up the receiver after William's call. She hadn't breakfasted or dressed yet. Shaken by William's information, she needed a moment to catch her breath, to digest what William had told her, to wake up.

Oh, my God!

She took a breath to settle herself.

So, Kimberly is home. I wonder why Warren didn't mention it to me. Sometimes that man gets so wrapped up in his work!

She took a quick shower and hastily dressed. Stockings, shoes, coiffed hair, green dress, stole, hat and gloves. Her driver took her to Elgin and let her out of her automobile at the hospital's entrance. She looked up at the foreboding hospital building and noticed the irony of a sunny, blue sky day while she struggled with an uneasy feeling. Trepidation.

Upon entering the medical facility, she made her way through the building asking for directions until she found the hall where Warren's room was located. The smell of disinfectant annoyed Marguerite, increasing her anxiety. A difficulty – the nurses at the nurse's station would not let her see Warren unless she was family.

Undaunted, she found a way to sneak down the hall toward his room. The room's door was windowed at the top so she was able to peer inside. Her view was obstructed by a man wearing a nice suit and holding his fedora, who stood next to Warren's bed. She could barely make out the man's profile.

Oh my gosh! Mr. Tresling! Warren's lawyer. What is he doing here?

She heard a shout.

"Madam! Madam! You must leave at once!" A nurse was running down the hall towards her.

The commotion caught Mr. Tresling's ear. He opened the door, saw Mrs. Bowles and spoke to the nurse.

"It's quite alright, nurse. I'm Mr. Weatherspoon's attorney. It's alright for this lady to be here."

The nurse, seemingly placated, turned and walked away.

Marguerite focused on Warren as she hastened to his bedside. Mr. Tresling's heart wrenched as he watched her struggle with her anguish. He respectfully stepped aside and moved to the foot of Warren's bed observing the communication between them.

Must shoulder a responsibility to Warren and show I can handle things.

"Oh, Warren!" Marguerite wrapped her arms around him carefully, observant of the wires and tubes attached to his body.

He patted her arm, reassuringly.

She looked into his reddened eyes and saw his puffy, stressed face. Half his face looked unnatural; drooping oddly. His breathing was labored.

"Warren, what happened?"

He placed his hand over his heart.

Marguerite started to weep, and retrieving a hanky from her purse, dabbed her eyes.

Warren looked at Mr. Tresling. The lawyer understood his unspoken message.

"Mrs. Bowles, Warren and I would like to have a talk with you. You see, some decisions need to be made and Mr. Weatherspoon has made it clear he wants you to be part of this discussion. Are you able to handle that right now?"

Marguerite straightened up, lifted her chin resolutely, and gave both men a nod. She sighed as they watched her collect herself.

"I understand. Tell me," she said.

Mr. Tresling cleared his throat and used simple words in this emotional setting. "We need to discuss Kimberly in the event Mr. Weatherspoon is no longer with us."

Marguerite looked at him, and then at Warren. Warren's unaffected eye clearly conveyed that this was a practical discussion not an emotional one.

"Warren has always been on top things, Mr. Tresling. I'm not surprised."

"Very good, Madam. There are several options. One option is to write a Will right now and have you witness it. Warren's estate will go to Kimberly. The concern is Kimberly is not capable of taking on that responsibility."

"I agree," Marguerite nodded.

"Another option is for you to assume Mr. Weatherspoon's estate. This agreement includes you taking responsibility for Kimberly for the rest of her life. The down side of this legal contract is a response from adversaries who might litigate in an effort to assume some or all of his assets."

"That would be worry-some, wouldn't it, Mr. Tresling?"

"That is correct, Mrs. Bowles. Mr. Weatherspoon's business associates are sometimes treacherous. Other times distant relatives appear and make a claim."

Marguerite saw where this discussion was headed. *Alright.*

"I assume you have a more preferable option, Mr. Tresling."

She looked at Warren again and saw assurance.

"Indeed, Mrs. Bowles. Marriage."

She gasped even though she expected the outcome. Too blunt.

I somehow felt I would marry Warren one day but I didn't think it would happen like this.

"I agree," she replied. "I agree to be Warren's wife, to assume responsibility for Kimberly, Warrens estate and," she paused for affect, "and also William." She faced Warren again. "He's been good to you, Warren, like family. I'll make sure he's well provided for."

Tresling and Marguerite saw Warren look up at the ceiling, disengaging from them for a moment, but also reflective. A single tear ran down the side of his face onto his pillow. Then he looked at Marguerite with an expression of gratitude.

* * *

OBITUARY

Mr. Warren Willard Weatherspoon passed away suddenly on November 25, 1942. The cause of his death was heart attack. He is survived by wife, Marguerite Lynn Bowles Wetherspoon, and daughter, Kimberly Luc Weatherspoon.

Mr. Warren Weatherspoon was well known for his business acumen in both the steel and railroad industries. His philanthropic contributions have been a hallmark to Chicago and surrounding counties. He will be missed.

CHAPTER FORTY-TWO
Burial
1942

Even the weather was melancholy. The gray sky produced a drizzle over rich green grass. A floral cascade of dark red roses had been draped over the steel casket. Marguerite thought the steel a metaphor to Warren's railroad and steel business. The gray casket was William's idea. It had scrolling on the sides and brass corners. Very masculine.

Kimberly shivered, her arms crossed over her torso hugging herself. She stood restlessly swaying to and fro as if to keep her blood circulating. Marguerite tightened a stole of mink pelts around her neck. The mink dressed her otherwise dark gray wool coat. This was not her favorite garment because it was heavy but it kept her warm. Mr. Tresling and William stood solemnly. Their wool neck scarves had been neatly tucked under their black wool coats. Everyone held umbrellas and wore galoshes. Even William, who was standing next to the Presbyterian Pastor. As was his duty, William held his umbrella over the Pastor's black fedora while his own fedora collected water on the brim. When the brim filled with water or when William bowed his head, a stream of water fell to the ground.

Marguerite couldn't decide whether her impatience had to do with Warren's agnostic views or the showcasing event now taking place. Previously, William had convinced her to have a short service at the burial site. His argument was based on social propriety.

When the service ended, Mr. Tresling gave his condolences to each person. Marguerite was impressed with his consideration of William. Then he excused himself and left. The minister escorted Marguerite to her car. Kimberly and William followed them.

The ride home was silent with each person lost in their own thoughts. William driving the car, wondered why Kimberly did not cry at her father's burial. Marguerite felt relieved that everything had been done.

* * *

Later, Marguerite sat in the drawing room with a bourbon and water. She recalled the pressure she felt over Warren's death. Thankfully, Tresling had helped with complicated legal matters over Warren's business agreements and his estate.

And she remembered William's insistence on decorum even though Warren's business associates had not been invited to the burial service. It was his point of view that convinced her. "A funeral is inappropriate for Mr. Weatherspoon. People who knew him would surly see the hypocritical gesture of a church service. No. A private burial service is best. It's what Mr. Weatherspoon would have wanted for you, Mrs. Weatherspoon."

William was right. And he was right about public scrutiny of Kimberly from curious people who may do her harm.

She gave a sigh of relief knowing it was in the past now.

She propped her feet up on the couch where she sat. Her dress, black full skirt with hidden pockets draped over her legs. She had removed the small cap with black netting. It was placed on a side table. Her thick hair had been braided into a bun.

William suddenly appeared. "May I have a few words with you, Mrs. Weatherspoon?"

She observed his resolute expression. "Of course, William. What's on your mind?"

William stood behind a padded cloth covered chair facing Mrs. Weatherspoon. "I've watched this family from the shadows of servitude, Mrs. Weatherspoon. I saw Kimberly develop into a woman. Her difficulty was much like mine in its intensity. There's fire in her that had to be controlled, whereas for me, I needed confidentiality and discretion. Ahem...."

Marguerite waited patiently.

"It's important to know who I am, Mam. I am a gentleman who desires the intimate company (a pause) of men."

"I'm not surprised," she replied. The fingers of her right hand toyed with her lower lip as a way to expend her nervous energy. Then she shifted her legs with her feet to the floor and leaned forward in her seat as she watched him look away from her. She waited while he tossed around his thoughts.

"There is another thing you should know." Ahem.... He shuffled his feet. "Mr. Weatherspoon had a similar interest in my proclivity."

Marguerite gasped as she turned red, her eyebrows raised. "I'm not sure I know what you mean, William." She pondered. *Proclivity... proclivity for sex?* "You and Mr. Weatherspoon?" Her jaw dropped as she fondled an earring on her right earlobe.

"Only a few times, Mrs. Weatherspoon. It was an experience. Something different. And I.... ahem.... Well you see Mam, I didn't mind .... too much."

She fell back against the cloth padding of the couch. William waited.

"Well.... Well.... I guess I'm not surprised. Ahem.... I knew he had dalliances. I didn't think it could be...."

William interrupted her. "Mrs. Weatherspoon, it's in the past."

"William, then why did you tell me?"

"I told you for both of us, Mam. You need to know the truth and I need to put it in the past. I loved Mr. Weatherspoon, too. I was his butler, confidant, problem handler, organizer, I was many things in this house."

Hmmm... truth... He's right.

"Indeed. Maybe at some level I knew this, William. Maybe not 'knew' but suspected something."

William raised his eyebrows with surprise, "What gave it away?"

"It was your attention to detail on subjects familiar to women. The artistic folding of napkins placed at a dinner setting. Your fuss over petite butter plates and butter knives. Color coordination. Floral arrangements. Concern for Kimberly and the secrets you have kept. You are good at these things because it pleases you. These are the things you have done to bring harmony into Warren's house. You were a partner and you stayed behind the scenes."

He searched into his top coat pocket, produced a handkerchief and dabbed his eyes. "Kimberly helped," he whispered.

"I'm sure she did when she could fit it into her schedule. Most of the time it was you, William."

"It's nice of you to have noticed, Mam."

She gave William a warm smile and tilted her head, "Is there anything else, William? Any other surprises I should know?"

Marguerites expression and gesture made him laugh. "No. I think you know everything now."

"Then please sit down." Marguerite indicated the comfortable cloth padded chair facing her. He replaced his handkerchief into his pocket and sat with his hands on his knees.

"So, William what do you make of all this?"

"Of what, Mam? The house, the burial or Miss Kimberly?"

"Kimberly."

"Well, Mrs. Weatherspoon, I see the consequences of Kimberly's stepping outside her station in life." He felt more comfortable so, he leaned back into his chair and placed his hands on the chair's arms.

"History has been against women like her. Joan of Arc, a warrior burned at the stake. Accusations of witches in Salem. In this era, it's woman's suffrage, Mam. It's still a man's world. Men in power can make things happen. As a man I shudder to think of what could have happened to me if someone detected my personal preference in privacy."

She appreciated William's candor. "Yes, I see that too. You are well spoken, William. How is that so?"

"I was studying to be a priest, Mrs. Weatherspoon. I read and study many things."

"What made you leave the priesthood?"

"A compromising set of circumstances that cast me out of the Catholic diocese. I sought servitude in a different venue."

Marguerite smiled inside not wanting to reveal her distaste of the Catholic faith. She had, already, accepted William's homosexuality. Now it was a desired feature in a house dominated by women.

"Mam, what IS to become of Miss Kimberly?"

"Good question, William, which is why I wanted to talk to you too. I think it's best Kimberly and I move away. Start a new life. We'll go east. Perhaps Virginia or maybe Maryland. Somewhere it's green, beautiful, and close to Washington D.C. There are advantages in the nation's Capital we can enjoy."

"And prospects for Kimberly, if possible, Mam."

"Exactly, William." They both thought, a*nd no one will know her past.*

"What if she becomes ill again, Mrs. Weatherspoon?"

"Yes, I thought of that. There's St. Elizabeth's Hospital," she replied.

"Oh. Is that like Elgin State Mental Hospital?"

"Yes. St. Elizabeth's has the best hospital services in the area so I think it could be a good facility for Kimberly, if needed.

She lowered her eyes and swirled her drink to take a moment. He waited until she looked at him again.

"I promised Warren I would take care of you. Your devotion to Warren and Kimberly has not gone unnoticed. You have a unique talent for anticipating what is needed and you are discrete. What you have, William, is rare. More than once Warren told me how much he appreciated you."

William was taken aback. His eyes watered again. He retrieved his handkerchief, dabbed his eyes and blew his nose. Marguerite turned her eyes away to give him a moment of privacy while he collected himself.

"Thank you, Mrs. Weatherspoon," he finally said and stuffed the handkerchief away. "Mr. Weatherspoon was not a man drawn to overt demonstrations of endearment."

She gave out a hearty laugh, "Indeed." He chuckled back.

Marguerite sighed. "I offer you two choices." She retrieved an envelope from her skirt pocket and handed it to him. While William opened the envelope, she continued. "The other offer, William, is to stay with us. Kimberly and I. The three of us can make a new future."

William's eyes fell upon the dollar amount clearly typed on the paper, forty-five thousand dollars and then the phrases 'termination of your extraordinary service' and 'pension from the Weatherspoon estate'.

"That's very generous, Mrs. Weatherspoon. May I take a day to think this over?"

"Of course," Marguerite replied.

Just then Kimberly came into the room. She was still dressed in her black mourning clothes but without her coat, hat and gloves. Her dress was closely fitted to her body so that a back slit was designed to allow her to walk freely. The top four buttons of her dress were loosened revealing her décolleté.

"May I interrupt?" she asked as she headed towards them.

"Yes, of course, dear. William and I were just talking about the burial. Please sit down and join us."

She sashayed to a cloth stuffed chair situated by William and crossed her legs when she sat down. She sat straight, her disposition regal but not spoiled. She laid her hands on her lap. There was something familiar about her and also something that had changed.

The pause became awkward as William and Marguerite watched Kimberly settle into her chair. They both thought the same thing. *Not as haughty as before.*

Marguerite broke the silence. "This is probably a good time to talk about the future, don't you think?"

William and Kimberly looked at each other and nodded.

"Kimberly, I've asked William to stay with us. He's thinking about it."

"OH," she replied with a shock. Looking at William, she said, "I don't know what I would do without you, William!"

William wondered how much she remembered of their past relationship. He had been watching over her for many years, careful not to step on Mr. Weatherspoon's toes. Warren never acknowledged this and Kimberly hardly noticed, so subtle was William's guardianship.

"Thank you, Miss Kimberly. That is very sweet." William reached out, held her hand and connected with her. "But I'm getting older. I'm just a couple years older than your father was. It's probably time for me to retire."

"Oh, William!" Kimberly's voice trembled and started to cry.

"There, there." Marguerite interjected. "Here's a fresh hanky." She retrieved it from her pocket and handed the linen to Kimberly, who took it and wiped her eyes. They both saw her struggle to keep from crying.

"This is too much, Marguerite," she pleaded. Then looking at William she offered, "You don't look old to me!"

William and Marguerite exchanged facial expressions.

Agreed this is too much. Too fast.

William spoke first, "I can stay for as long as you need me, Miss Kimberly. Please don't worry."

"Then it's settled, at least for a while now," Marguerite hastily replied. "William, what do you have for supper?"

"Oh, yes. Supper. How about something light. Salads. Cole slaw, potato salad, green bean salad, deviled eggs and biscuits."

"Sounds wonderful. Will you please serve supper in thirty minutes? I'd like to change clothes," Mrs. Weatherspoon said.

"Me too." Kimberly rose from her chair, walked towards the entry way, turned around and paused. Her eyes scanned the room, the cloth covered chairs, low tables scattered about, the bar and briefly settled on the curio cabinet. The items inside, carved ivory figurines, were different from what she had remembered.

What happened to the china dolls in Dresden Lace?

She shrugged her shoulders, headed towards the stairs, and paused at the first step. William and Marguerite watched her turn her head up towards the top landing. They sucked in their breath as a soft light briefly glimmered upon her face making her appear angelic. When she started her climb, the light had vanished.

Author's Notes

"The Fading of Kimberly" was inspired when researching my book, *"The Fading of Lloyd"*, which is about family secrets, truth and forgiveness. Lloyd, my uncle, died in a mental hospital.

Through my research, I found mental illness a huge problem that will probably never be unraveled. Mired in the unique elements of individual cases, it is an infinite problem set, where we muddle through volume and detail as best we can.

Initial attempts at unraveling the puzzle was categorization of symptoms. The book, *"The Mask of Insanity"* talks about this strategy in the early twentieth century; delightfully written using jargon of that era. We now have DMS5, which is the standard classification of mental disorders used today.

"Madness in Civilization", is an encyclopedia of how patients with mental illnesses were treated throughout history and is well researched. Some of the solutions discussed in this book are shocking (no pun intended). Doctors used strategies that were not fully vetted – certainly not by our twenty-first century standards. The moral imperative is explored.

"Mad in America, Bad Science, Bad Medicine, and the Enduring Mistreatment of the Mentally Ill" reinforces the difficulty in finding cures, while balancing the rights of the patient. When can mentally infirm persons speak for themselves? This book explores what had happened.

"Mental Ills and Bodily Cures" surprised me with its statistical evidence of gender bias when choosing lobotomy as a cure for "socially unacceptable behavior" disguised in a prognosis of mental infirmity. I recall the story Rosemary Kennedy, sister to President John F. Kennedy, and Senators Robert F. Kennedy and Ted Kennedy, whose life forever changed after her lobotomy. Kimberly's story is similar.

On the flip side of the problem is the viewpoint of prisons, insane asylums and mental health institutions. How can the right people be found to work in a mental institution or a prison? How can assault be prevented when the facility is characterized by people in a position of power over others who are powerless? How can one effectively manage the population? These are Dr. Reed's difficulties.

I sincerely hope the reader has become more aware of the challenges we face in the conundrum of mental illness and institutions whose purpose is to help, but sometimes falls short of helping in a meaningful way.

WHAT'S TRUE

Unless otherwise indicated, everything in this book is fictional. However, some things are based on truth.

Elgin State Hospital

Elgin State Hospital was established in 1869. It answered a growing need as Americans moved westward through the new country.

The front of the main building of Elgin State Hospital was 1,086 feet long, an impressive entrance that commanded respect. Over time the facility grew to include annex buildings for female patients, war veterans, the symptomatic destitute, people with dementia, recovering addicts and alcoholics, doctor's offices, and housing for hospital staff living on the premises. By 1910, the hospital had 1200 beds.

During the 1930s and 40s, the estate had a nursing school, pharmaceutical lab, hydrotherapy and occupational therapy services, and a farm colony, complete with hogs, horses, chickens, dairy barn, slaughter house, and agricultural grounds.

Elgin State Hospital had its own water tower and power plant. In its hay-day, soon after WWII, the size of the estate was 1,139 acres.

Elgin State Hospital **did not** have a prison-like facility to accommodate the criminally insane. Few mental hospitals had such resources in the early twentieth century, even though the need existed to treat the criminally insane. My purpose for creating 'The Hold' was to demonstrate the singular need and the difficulties faced in handling extreme cases. Toward that end, I thought it a creative idea for Dr. Nigel Reed to reach out to the academic communities to help the patient or gain progress in a study of the problem. I also wanted to show psychology, psychiatry, and criminology thinking during that era.

The events in this story represent the kinds of things that have happened in many mental institutions during the early twentieth century.

The Superintendent of Elgin State Hospital from 1930 to 1946 was Dr. Charles F. Read. He was a leader in neurology and a proponent of chemical shock therapy (see obituary in Chicago Tribune March 12, 1946). Dr. Read signed the death certificate of my uncle, Lloyd Huttleston, whose story is told in my book, The Fading of Lloyd.

https://en.wikipedia.org/wiki/Elgin_Mental_Health_Center

Chicago Mayor 'Big Bill' Thompson

'Big Bill' (a.k.a. William Hale Thompson) served three terms as a Republican Mayor of Chicago. He was quite a character, having his own speakeasy – a boat that eventually sunk due to too much weight. His political debate using rats is true. He had disdain for King George V; probably used as a humorous talking point that gave him notoriety (*my speculation*). He also had associations with organized crime. As of this writing, he was the last Republican to serve as Mayor of Chicago.

https://en.wikipedia.org/wiki/William_Hale_Thompson

Tony Accardo

Tony Accardo was affiliated with Al Capone, taking care of Capone's interests while the gangster served time in jail for tax evasion. He had a wife named Clarice.

https://en.wikipedia.org/wiki/Timeline_of_organized_crime_in_Chicago

Thomas Malloy

Thomas Malloy was killed on February 4, 1935. He was president of local 110 of the Motion Picture Operators Union. The FBI believed Tony Accardo was involved in this hit.

https://en.wikipedia.org/wiki/Timeline_of_organized_crime_in_Chicago

The No Name Club and Simon Lundberg

The 'No Name Club' and Simon Lundberg are based on a true story. Simon was a Swedish immigrant that opened a speakeasy in the 1920's. He really did cash checks for his patrons on payday Friday. The establishment is now a restaurant in suburban Chicago.

The description of the establishment and the robbery are conjecture.

https://www.chibarproject.com/Reviews/Simon%27s/Simon%27s.htm

Prisons and Mental Hospitals in the Early Twentieth Century

The problem of handling psychopathic patients and the criminally insane has been a conundrum, balancing ethics, protection of society and treating the mentally infirm. Today, criminal psychopaths end up in prisons such as the Massachusetts Correctional Institution at Bridgewater (MCIB).

https://en.wikipedia.org/wiki/Bridgewater_State_Hospital

Memorial Day Massacre

Ten people were shot by police during a steel strike on Memorial Day, as mentioned in the chapter "Viking Trouble".

https://en.wikipedia.org/wiki/Memorial_Day_massacre_of_1937

The New Moon

The new moon dates, as depicted in this novel, are true.

It turns out there really was a book, "Emily of New Moon" by L.M. Montgomery. How convenient!

There really was a solar eclipse observed in the early morning across Illinois on Saturday, January 25, 1925.

Elgin Watch Factory

The Elgin Watch Factory had an observatory that was used to precisely set their watches. My description of the facility is conjecture.

https://en.wikipedia.org/wiki/Elgin_National_Watch_Company. See also "Elgin Time: Elgin National Watch Company" by Bill Briska.

Eugenics

Early twentieth century belief in eugenics was prevalent throughout America and Europe. The idea has laid the foundation for racial, gender and cultural bias, as well as treatment of the mentally infirm and justification for sterilization.

For example, a mentally infirmed woman, in the early twentieth century, living in a mental institution, had an eighty percent chance of being given a lobotomy. (see the chapter "Discipline Gendered: Women and the Practice of Lobotomy" in the book, Mental Ills and Bodily Cures by Joel Baslow.)

Other good sources on this subject are:

http://knowgenetics.org/history-of-eugenics/
Mad in America by Robert Whitaker
Madness in Civilization by Andrew Scull

Havelock Ellis

Dr. Havelock Ellis, an intellectual during the early twentieth century, studied human sexuality. He co-authored a book regarding homosexuality and recognized transgender issues. He demonstrated an interest in narcissism (a subject of this book) that eventually became part of psychoanalysis.

https://en.wikipedia.org/wiki/Havelock_Ellis

Joliet Prison and Warden Joseph Ragen

Joseph Ragen was the Warden of Joliet Correctional Center in the early twentieth century. He is credited for being a successful, strict administer in a prison that held the worst criminals.

Joliet prison has a bumpy history with dilapidated facilities, prison unrest, riots, murders and escapes. It was opened in 1858 and closed in 2002. Famous criminals include Nathan Leopold and Richard Loeb, who were students that killed on a whim and a dare, believing they could get away with the crime.

The description of the prison is conjecture.

http://www.saturdayeveningpost.com/wp-content/uploads/satevepost/18915626.pdf
https://en.wikipedia.org/wiki/Joliet_Correctional_Center

Greta Garbo and Mr. Lubitsch

Greta Garbo was a talented Swedish-American actress who worked with director Mr. Lubitsch in the film *"Ninotchka"*. The party scene is totally conjecture and way too much fun.

London After Midnight

The movie, *"London After Midnight"*, is true. Sadly, no remaining copies of this classic horror film exists.

By MGM - ha.com, Public Domain, https://commons.wikimedia.org/w/index.php?curid=38121244
https://en.wikipedia.org/wiki/London_After_Midnight_(film)

The Perfect Ratio

Sometimes referred to as the "Golden Ratio", it truly is the proportion as to what we think is "beautiful" (aesthetically pleasing). The value of the "Golden Ratio" is 1.618 to 1. It's represented by the Greek letter Phi.

Anne Boleyn

She was the second wife of King Henry VIII. Her right hand had six fingers.

* * *

WHAT'S FALSE

Roache Boarding School

Roache Boarding School is fictional. The institution serves my purpose to depict societal views and expectations of females in the early twentieth century.

Bibliography

Boskey, Elizabeth, Harper, Judith, and Hilgenkamp, Kathryn. *The Truth About Rape, Second Edition,* Fact on File, Inc., An Imprint of InfoBase Publishing, New York, 2010.

Bowen, Murray. *Family Therapy in Clinical Practice.* Jason Aronson, Inc., 1982.

Braslow, Joel. *Mental Ills and Bodily Cures, Psychiatric Treatment in the First Half of the Twentieth Century.* University of California Press, 1997.

Cohen, Adam. *Imbeciles, The Supreme Court, American Eugenics, and the Sterilization of Carrie Buck.* Penguin Press, 2016.

Oakley, Barbara. *Evil Genes: Why Rome Fell, Hitler Rose, Enron Failed and My Sister Stole My Mother's Boyfriend.* Prometheus Books, New York, 2008.

Jung, C.G. *The Archetypes and the Collective Unconscious.* Second Edition. Princeton University Press, 1968.

Scull, Andrew. *Madness in Civilization.* Princeton University Press, 2015.

Toman, Walter. *Family Constellation.* Springer Publishing Company, Inc., New York, 1976.

Whitaker, Robert. *Mad in America, Bad Science, Bad Medicine, and the Enduring Mistreatment of the Mentally Ill.* Basic Books, a member of the Perseus Books Group, Philadelphia, Pennsylvania, 2010.

Movies:

"The Snake Pit" (1948) – book by Mary Jane Ward. Movie produced by 20th Century Fox with Olivia de Havilland as Virginia Cunningham.

"Titicut Follies" (1967) – movie about stark conditions of treatment of the mentally insane at Bridgewater State Hospital.

Web Links:

Asylum Projects, whose purpose is to archive both historical and current information on asylums across the United States and around the world. http://www.asylumprojects.org/index.php?title=Elgin_State_Hospital

Bridgewater State Hospital is a facility specifically for the criminally insane. https://en.wikipedia.org/wiki/Bridgewater_State_Hospital

DSM-5, Diagnostic and Statistical Manual of Mental Disorders. https://en.wikipedia.org/wiki/DSM-5

Greenstein Act: The Need for a New Approach for Psychopathic Criminals   http://scholarship.law.upenn.edu/cgi/viewcontent.cgi?article=7758&context=penn_law_review

About Kit Crumpton

Kit Crumpton, a historical novelist, is the author of *Raiding the Empire of the Sun: Tinian 1945* (2015) about B-29 Superfortress missions over Japan during WWII. The main character is based on her father. Her second book, *The Fading of Lloyd* (2017) is based upon her uncle who was mentally challenged. Her third book, *The Fading of Kimberly* (2018) is a story of the mentally and physically disadvantaged who were institutionalized during the early twentieth century. Kit believes a good book teaches history through story telling. Find her online at KitCrumpton.com.